THE RAMBLERS' ASSOCIATION

WALKS IN THE COUNTRYSIDE ROUND BRISTOL

THE RAMBLERS' ASSOCIATION

WALKS IN THE COUNTRYSIDE ROUND BRISTOL

W. Foulsham & Co. Ltd.
London · New York · Toronto · Cape Town · Sydney

The Ramblers' Association

1–5 Wandworth Road
London SW8 2LJ
Tel: 01 582 6878

796.52

44430

W. Foulsham & Company Limited

Yeovil Road, Slough, Berkshire, SL1 4JH

ISBN 0-572-01316-7

Photoset in Great Britain by C. R. Barber and Partners
(Highlands) Ltd., Fort William, Scotland

Printed in Great Britain at St. Edmundsbury Press, Bury St.
Edmunds.

Cover: Castle Combe (Walk 15)

INFORMATION ABOUT THE RAMBLERS' ASSOCIATION

The Ramblers' Association is a registered charity with three main aims.
- to protect footpaths and other rights of way and increase access to open country.
- to defend outstanding landscapes.
- to encourage people to walk in the countryside.

It carries out these aims at a national level, through the employment of staff to run national campaigns, lobby MPs, etc. and generally organise the work of the Association, and at a local level through the activities of the voluntary workers in its Areas and Groups, who tackle problems on paths, both by reporting them to highway authorities and by carrying out practical work, such as stile building and waymaking. The Areas and Groups also have programmes of rambles and other events.

Since it was formed in 1935 the RA has grown steadily, and in 1984 membership topped 44,000 for the first time. The RA's branch structure has also developed, in particular through the formation of local Groups within Areas.

The threats to the countryside and its paths are growing, and so are our needs. You can help simply by becoming a member. There are plenty of opportunities for joining in the practical footpath and amenity work carried out by your local RA Group.

As a member you will be able to take advantage of the following benefits.

■ **A local group** to walk with (but go on your own if you prefer); most groups run social events too. ■ Free annual **Bed and Breakfast Guide** with more than 2,000 addresses where walkers are welcome. ■ **Rucksack,** the RA's own magazine, plus your own area news, four times a year. ■ Use of our 1:50,000 Ordnance Survey map library. ■ **Discounts** in more than 100 outdoor equipment shops. ■ **Special offers on publications;** a discount subscription to **The Great Outdoors** magazine. ■ Access to our national service of **expert advice and information.**

PROTECTING THE
FOOTPATH HERITAGE

INTRODUCTION

The information given below is about the law relating to public rights of way in England and Wales.

Public paths are highways in law. They have the same legal protection in principle as metalled carriageways, the difference being that paths are dedicated to use by limited classes of traffic, i.e. walkers on footpaths; and walkers, riders and cyclists on bridleways.

An old legal maxim says that once a highway always a highway. This means that a public path can only be closed by statutory procedure. It does not cease to be a right of way simply because it is unused or little used.

HOW YOU CAN HELP

Paths are part of our heritage and need our protection. Every time you walk along a path you help to keep it open. By varying routes to include little known paths and by reporting any difficulties you meet you can make every step count in the struggle to preserve our country walks.

Reporting difficulties. Write to the appropriate local authority (see below) and tell the RA. Give location (six figure grid reference) and nature of problem, path number and name of owner or tenant (if known). RA national office will supply you with obstruction report forms ready for use.

Obstructions. An obstruction is anything which hinders your free passage along the path, e.g. a barbed wire fence where there should be a gap or stile. County councils have a statutory duty to keep public paths open for public use and enjoyment.

Ploughing. It is illegal to plough a path along a field boundary. The farmer is required to leave room between the hedge or fence and the cultivated area for the path. Paths going across fields may be ploughed, provided that the farmer restores the path within two weeks of ploughing. Report infringements to county or district councils.

Bridges and overgrowth. A missing bridge or overgrowth on the surface of the path are within the highway authority's maintenance responsibilities. The highway authorities are the county councils but some district councils have taken over maintenance from the counties. Overgrowth from the sides of the path should be dealt with by the owner or tenant of the land. The highway authority has power to act if he does not.

Misleading notices, i.e. any signs which by false or misleading information may deter people from using a public path, are an offence on paths shown on the definitive map. Report to highway authority.

Bulls. No bull over the age of ten months is allowed to be at large on its own in a field crossed by a public path, and no bull of a recognised dairy breed (Ayrshire, British Friesian, British Holstein, Dairy Shorthorn, Guernsey, Jersey and Kerry) is allowed in such a field under any circumstances. It is not a specific offence for beef and cross breed bulls to be at large in fields crossed by public paths if they are accompanied by cows or heifers, but if the bull endangers public safety an offence may be committed under section 3 of the Health and Safety at Work Act 1974. Report any problems to the police.

PRACTICAL WORK

Increasingly, branches of the RA and local footpath and amenity societies are undertaking practical work to improve the condition of the paths.

This takes two main forms: path clearance and waymarking. Waymarking is carried out by painting arrows at points along the path where the route is unclear.

FURTHER READING

A brief exposition of the law in England and Wales is contained in a leaflet published by the RA, *Right of Way*. The RA also publishes, in conjunction with the Open Spaces Society, *Rights of Way: a Guide to Law and Practice*, a comprehensive 368-page book which includes the text of the relevant legislation. The RA also sells *Footpaths: a practical handbook* published by the British Trust for Conservation Volunteers, which is a most comprehensive guide to practical work.

CONTENTS

These walks have been compiled by members of the Ramblers' Association and its affiliated societies.

The maps

The sketch maps in this book are meant to be used in conjunction with the Ordnance Survey map mentioned at the beginning of each walk. Symbols on the maps have been simplified and are meant to give rough guidance to the location of symbols on the Ordnance Survey map.

Symbols used

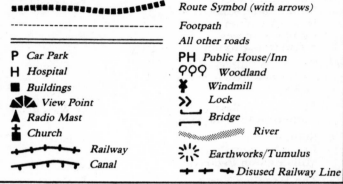

■■■■■■■■■■■■■■■■■■	*Route Symbol (with arrows)*
-----------------------------	*Footpath*
══════════════════	*All other roads*
P *Car Park*	**PH** *Public House/Inn*
H *Hospital*	♀♀♀ *Woodland*
■ *Buildings*	✸ *Windmill*
◣◪ *View Point*	≫ *Lock*
▲ *Radio Mast*	⊔ *Bridge*
✝ *Church*	*River*
┿┿┿┿┿ *Railway*	⁂ *Earthworks/Tumulus*
⁀⁀⁀ *Canal*	✛ ✛ ✛ *Disused Railway Line*

14

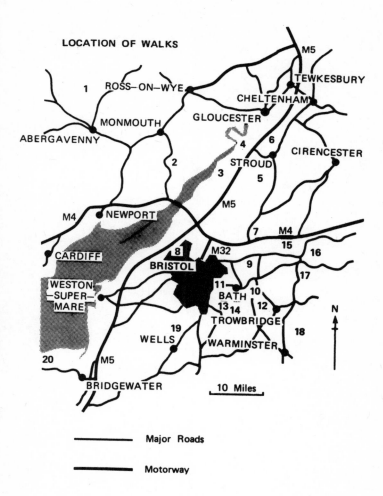

LOCATION OF WALKS

1 ROSS–ON–WYE
MONMOUTH
ABERGAVENNY
2
M4 NEWPORT
CARDIFF
WESTON–SUPER–MARE
20 M5
BRIDGEWATER

M5 TEWKESBURY
CHELTENHAM
GLOUCESTER
4 6 CIRENCESTER
3 STROUD
5
M5
7 M4
15
16
8 M32
BRISTOL
9
17
11 10
BATH
13 14 12
TROWBRIDGE
19 18
WELLS WARMINSTER

N

10 Miles

—————— Major Roads

▬▬▬▬▬▬ Motorway

WALK 1 THE BLACK MOUNTAINS LLANTHONY–PARTRISHOW– LLANTHONY

DESCRIPTION:	Visiting the southern end of the Black Mountains. A varied walk of hill and valley, of contrasting scenery and visiting the historic church of Partrishow. Fine distant views.
MAPS:	OS 1:50,000 Sheet 161 (Abergavenny and Black Mountains).
	OS 1:25,000 Brecon Beacons Leisure Map – Eastern Area.
DISTANCE:	12 miles.
TERRAIN:	Easy tracks through forest, good tracks over or on edge of moorland, steep rough descent into/out of Llanthony, otherwise easy to moderate gradients.
FOOD AND DRINK:	Llanthony Abbey Hotel (normal pub hours, afternoon tea to 5.00 p.m.) 'Half Moon' Inn (food).
TRANSPORT:	None available.
START AND FINISH:	Llanthony Abbey car park.

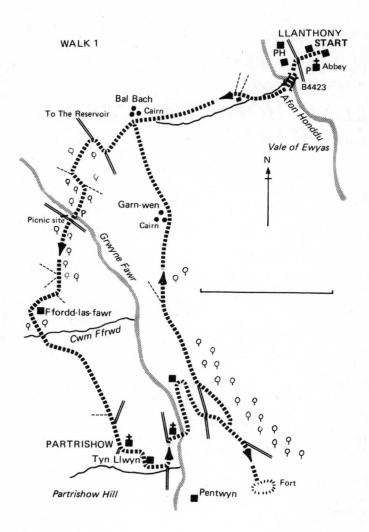

WALK 1

Start out from **Llanthony Abbey car park** (Grid Ref SO 288278) in the Vale of Ewyas. From the car park walk down the road towards the 'village'. Take the lane past the cottage **(The Mill)** signposted Bal Bach 2 km. The way up on to the mountain is waymarked, but a description follows. Cross the stream over the steel footbridge, take the stile on your right, walk up the side of the field, over the next stile, and cross a muddy lane to a gate, labelled 'way to mountain, follow stream'. Continue up through scattered trees to a wooden footbridge over the stream. Cross this and continue up, with stream now on your left to a small wicket gate. Pass through up to a farmyard. Pass through two iron gates and bear left around the corner of the building. Follow the waymarked route up the line of the coombe over three stiles. At the third stile meet a track coming in from the right. Continue up above the coombe on a rough track to the cairn at **Bal Bach** on the ridge crest. Descend straight down the hillside on a rough track, and turn right at the meeting of a level track contouring above the forest. After about 200 yards, go left through a gate into the forest. Go down the forestry track, bear left, on the level, and then right to continue the descent to the picnic site and car park for Myndd Ddu forest. Cross the road and bear left at a slant up a gently-rising forestry track. At junction of tracks bear hard left, and then go round the bend to a gate. Pass through this, and continue on to a disused farm, now a holiday home, **Ffordd-las-fawr.** Pass through the yard and through the gate into a wood. Leave the wood by a wicket gate and go over the stream. Continue along a broad track above fields, with open hillside on your right, to meet a gate leading into more enclosed track. Note the superb views of the valley and ridge along this section. Next, pass through the gate on to a tarmac road. Follow this bearing right, to the church of **Partrishow.** The road descends sharply to the coombe; part-way down, a stile leads into the churchyard.

Partrishow church dates from about 1150. Nearby is the cell of St. Issui; the well of St. Issui (St. Mary's Well) is situated by the roadside as it crosses the side-stream of Nant Mair, just below the church. There have been several name variations; Parttrissw (15th century), Llanysho or Partrisso (1555), Partrishow (1721) and Partricio (1793) (the most recent). The valley road was once the main route from Abergavenny to Talgarth. In the church note the Tudor road-screen and a mural of Time, a figure bearing a scythe.

Leave the churchyard by a kissing-gate at the east end into a field. Follow the track which loops down to the farm of **Tyn Llwyn.**

This farm is of historical interest having once been inhabited by the Herbert family of Pembroke Castle, who intermarried with the Vaughans of Tretower Court near Crickhowell.

Pass through the farmyard to the road. Then bear left at the road for about 500 yards. Turn right at the road fork, and go past the

Baptist Church (1837), over the river and up the road ascending to a farm. At the end of the farm outbuilding bear right up a rough track, pass through a gate and on up to a gate leading on to the ridge top. Go over the gate on to the open hill, cross the track ahead, and continue on to the ridge crest, with a wall on your right. The ridge ahead leads to the conspicuous **Iron Age hill fort** which terminates the ridge, and from which good views are obtained in all directions, particularly across to Sugar Loaf mountain, and the conspicuous landslip above Cwmyoy.

From the hill fort, note below the sudden divergence of the courses of the Honddu to the north-east and Grwyne Fawr to the south-west; previously they were parallel. This is due to a large moraine, left as the glaciers of the Ice Age retreated, to the south and south-west of Llanvihangel Crucorney.

Retrace your steps along the ridge in a northerly direction, now keeping to the ridge top with fine panoramic views into the whole of the Black Mountains. Pass a wood on the right, and then proceed along a wide trackway between two walls to a gate, where there is a waymark. The track widens, and the walls separate. Keep to the left hand wall; the ridge narrows somewhat. Pass a small stone pillar in mid-track, and at the fork of tracks on the ridge, bear right. The rising track goes between two walls with a wood on the right, then on to the open ridge. Follow this to a prominent pillar/cairn **(Garnwen)** and then on to Bal Bach where the outward route is joined. Bear right down the coombe and follow the track to the **Abbey,** now clearly in view, as on the start of the walk, which is waymarked through the field section.

Llanthony Abbey, now ruined, was founded in 1107 as an Augustinian priory. Across the car park is the parish church of St. David. Llanthony Abbey was bought by W. S. Landor, the poet in 1802, but he found it uncongenial. He did however plant groves of Spanish chestnuts. The valley of Grwyne Fawr once supported small paper mills and the whole area has been considerably de-populated over the last 150 years.

WALK 2 THE WYE VALLEY
TINTERN – TRELLECK – TINTERN

DESCRIPTION:	The walk takes one through a very unspoiled stretch of country, with historic and natural interest, well away from the crowds of the more popular areas of the Wye Valley.
MAPS:	OS 1:50,000 Sheet 171 (Cardiff & Newport); Sheet 162 (Forest of Dean). OS 1:25,000 SO 40/50 (St Briavels).
DISTANCE:	$12\frac{1}{2}$ miles.
TERRAIN:	Woodland, rolling hills, pleasant streams.
FOOD AND DRINK:	Trelleck, (Lion Inn) The Parkhouse Inn. Tintern: several hotels; refreshments for tea and soft drinks. Trelleck Grange (Fountains Inn).
TRANSPORT:	Bus: 'Wyevale' (Nat Bus Co) – 49 Chepstow-Tintern-Monmouth; every 2 hours 9 a.m.–6 p.m. 50 Chepstow-Trelleck-Monmouth; infrequent Mon.–Fri., 1 bus Saturdays, none Sundays.
START AND FINISH:	Tintern Abbey car park.

WALK 2

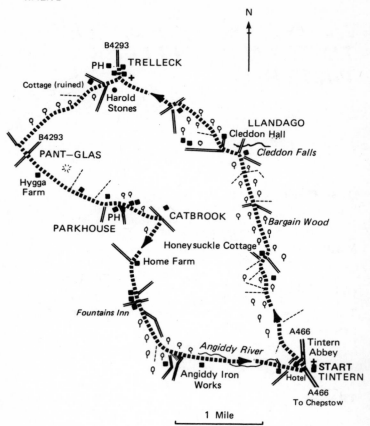

N

B4293
PH ■ ▪ TRELLECK
Cottage (ruined) ✝
        Harold
        Stones
        B4293
    PANT-GLAS
Hygga
Farm
        PH ■   ▪ CATBROOK
PARKHOUSE
            Honeysuckle Cottage
            Home Farm

LLANDAGO
Cleddon Hall
        ▪ Cleddon Falls

        Bargain Wood

Fountains Inn

            Angiddy River
        Angiddy Iron
        Works   A466
                        Tintern
                        Abbey
                        ✝ START
                    Hotel   TINTERN
                        A466
                        To Chepstow

1 Mile

22

Start from **Tintern Abbey** (SO 534001). From the Abbey car park, cross the cricket ground to the left at the Anchor Hotel, where there are public toilets, and come on to the main road opposite the **Royal George Hotel**. Continue along the main road for a few yards, and cross the road to take the track on the left, climbing steeply up into the woods. Public toilets are 10 yards further down the main road on the right. The track is signposted 'Whitelye 2.5 km'. A lane bears left at the foot of the climb; take the rough track bearing upwards to the right, which is virtually a stream bed under usual conditions, and is crossed by minor streamlets at several points. After some distance, a track comes in from the left. Bear right, now on level ground, with occasional views through the trees down to the Wye, until a sharp bend to the left is reached. A path goes to the right, back downhill. Do not take it. Pass round a superfluous gate to the left, and take the gently rising track, set between a bank and a low stone wall. Continue along this path with a leafy arch of foliage, and woods to the left, passing a small track off to the left, until it comes out into the open, and joins a track coming in from the right.

Continue straight on, passing a small outbuilding on the left, and reapproaching the woods, with views again to the Wye. Just after entering the stretch with woodland again on the left, go round a slight bend leftwards. An indistinct path goes downhill through the bracken and a young planting of conifers, just before the edge of the mature woodland on the right is reached. After 20 yards of descent, the path enters light deciduous woodland, and a further 10 yards on, meets tracks at right angles. Cross these and continue on the small path downhill, fairly steeply, with a hedge on the right, through the wood, to meet the end of a track at the entrance to a cottage. Turn left along this track, which winds through the woods to join a main forestry roadway. Bear right downhill along this to meet the road at **Honeysuckle Cottage**. The start of the indistinct path will probably be difficult to find shortly, as young trees mature, although it is on the map as a right of way. *An easier way may be to continue along the main track for just 10 yards, to a crossing of tracks. Bear right downhill along a main forestry road directly to Honeysuckle Cottage.*

At Honeysuckle Cottage, bear right down the road and turn up left at the junction ahead, for 1 mile, to the next junction, where there is good car parking space.

Here take the track, continuing in the same general direction, signposted, 'Footpath, Cleddon 1.2 km' and waymarked with a low post carrying a blue arrow. A wide gravel track marked by a yellow arrow goes off right to public toilets. This point is also an official picnic site. The smaller track following the blue arrow, goes straight on, rising steeply for 100 yards, then level, where it becomes a broad ride through the trees of **Bargain Wood**. After $\frac{1}{2}$ mile, a fork in tracks is reached. Ignore a previous track coming in from the left. Take the left-hand narrow green path, which continues on in the same general direction as before. It is waymarked by a small post carrying both a blue arrow and a yellow arrow and dot. The right-hand track goes to F.C. Stonehill, Tintern Forest. After a short distance the green path comes out into the open where it is joined by a track coming in from the left. Continue along what is now a track between low stone walls; the junction just mentioned is waymarked by a yellow arrow and dot on a post. As one walks along, views are now obtained over small paddocks and cottages to the Wye again. At a cross tracks, turn left. (The track straight on is waymarked by a yellow arrow and dot; it leads eventually to Cleddon Falls, and is part of the 'Wye Valley Walk'.) Almost immediately turn right, past **Rose Cottage,** to join the road. Here turn left and follow it for 400 yards to **Cleddon Hall.** Just past a disused entrance to the Hall, on the right, is an iron kissing gate, signposted; 'public footpath' into a field. Cross this diagonally and exit by a corresponding iron kissing gate, to the right of a more conspicuous wooden gate into a lane.

Turn right for 100 yards along this track, and then go left along a path leading into the woods. Follow this winding path, which soon runs past the remains of a stone wall on the left, to the edge of the wood, where there are several large slabs of natural rock which may afford a resting place to admire the view. Proceed down the path, skirting the garden of the bungalow, and so on to the road (signposted (back) to Cleddon 1.2 km).

Turn right, and follow the road for $1\frac{1}{2}$ miles to Trelleck. (Note on your right St. Mary Well, 400 yards short of the village.)

Trelleck boasts two inns. The Well is said to be curative and is iron impregnated. The tumulus in the area of Church Farm is possibly either a burial mound or the remains of the keep of a Norman Motte Castle. The Three Stones, so-called Harold Stones, just outside the village are earlier than King Harold. The village of Trelleck was once considerably larger, exceeding Chepstow and Monmouth in size in the 13th century. The church was endowed in the 7th and 8th century by local Kings of Gwent; the present building is 600 years old.

On leaving either of the village inns, turn right back in the direction of Chepstow.

At the road junctions at the end of the village by **Church Farm,** take the extreme right turn, B4293. In the field on the left are the Three Stones, and the tumulus can be seen as a bank in the area of the buildings of Church Farm. 300 yards down the road, turn right into a lane, and after a further 200 yards bear left past a disused cottage on the right. Go through a gate across the track, and up a slight rise into a field. Go through the gate on the left, down over the stream by a bridge, through a gate and up the rise into the next field. Bear right, with a fence on your right. Keep slightly up from the fence to a small hinged gate at the top end of the trees. Cross the edge of the next field, still with the fence on the right and thick woods down on the right in the valley, to a small gully. Cross this and exit by a small hinged gate into the next field. Pass around a small pond and along the side of the field to a small iron gate in the next cross-hedge. Pass along the edge of the next field with the hedge on the left, through a gate, along the edge of the next field and through a gate on to the metalled lane at **Pant-glas Farm.** From the vicinity of Pant-glas, good views are obtained across to the hills above the Pontypool area.

Walk up the lane to the B4293, and immediately cross it into the lane leading to **Hygga Farm,** signposted 'Parkhouse 1.8 km'. At Hygga, continue through a gate, and down a wide, rough lane, with fine views across the surrounding rolling countryside. At the bottom of the lane, turn left into a sunken lane by a gate, noting in passing the ancient settlement of **Ffynnon Gaer** up on the hillside to the left. The lane is usually also a small shallow stream bed, but with a firm bottom and frequent rock slabs which are slippery. Negotiate this for 100 yards; then turn right up a green lane. After 50 yards there is an electricity sub-station on the left. This becomes a semi-gravel track for $\frac{3}{4}$ mile, to a junction. Here turn left up a metalled road, for a short distance to crossroads, where the **Parkhouse Inn** is on the right. Go over the crossroads and follow the road towards Catbrook. Pass by the first lanes coming in on right to pair in a V. Turn right into the next lane by a telephone box. After 50 yards go left over an iron gate into a small path which widens out, past some buildings, and into a small field. Pass between a gap in the hedges, along the top of the field with a copse on the left, and cross the stile into the road. Immediately take a stile 5 yards down on your right into a field. Go down this with the hedge on the right to the next stile. There are fine views here over the hills. Continue down the hillside, with a wall and woodland on the right, through a small area of bracken and rough grazing to a stile in the wire fence ahead. (part of the 'Rough Grounds' on the map). Continue into the next field, across several (? temporary) wire fences to a small hedge on the left, by the side of the fence to the corner there is a stile in the hedge, and so on to the road. Turn left, past **Home Farm,** and road walk for $\frac{1}{2}$ mile to the **'Fountains' Inn.**

Go just past the Fountains Inn, and immediately take the track on your right, a concealed entrance hard by the fence screen of the Inn. Follow this to its end, go over the gate into the field, and continue along its top edge with the hedge on your right. Descend slightly into a partly sunken green track which still keeps to the top of the field.

Pass through a gap in the cross-hedge, continue along with very attractive views of valley and woods, past two upright stones, and descend to an iron gate leading on to the road. Turn left at the road junction just ahead, over the **Angiddy river** by a stone bridge, and turn left down towards Chapel Hill. Note the remains of attractive trout ponds to the right. Continue down the road for a short distance to **Angiddy Iron Works;** excavated and partly restored on the left. Viewing permits may be obtained from Tintern Railway Station – but they can be viewed adequately from the road.

Just opposite on the other side of the road is a wicket gate with a waymark on the other side. Go along the narrow path towards the cottage, not along the apparent path by the riverside. The path nearer the cottage bears left over the streamlet, and rises slightly to join a larger track. Bear left along this, which follows down the valley just above the river. Soon take a side track left, over the river to rejoin the road. Do not continue along the main track ahead.

Walk down the road to a side lane going off right, and over the river. Turn off into this and immediately after crossing river, take the narrow footpath by the side of the stream which is now on your left. Follow this past houses on to a wider well-kept grassy path between cottages and gardens and by the riverside down to the **'Cherry Tree' Inn,** which has a very pretty semi-covered patio, surrounded by cottage gardens. Rejoin the main valley road and walk down this for the last few yards back into **Tintern.**

On returning to the car park at Tintern Abbey, the Abbey ruins are probably too well known to need description here. However, the disused church of St. Mary up on the hill across the A466 is reached by a minor lane to the right of the garage on the A466, and then up a laid stone path. From it are good views of the Abbey, village and valley. Across the Wye is Abbey Passage Farm, named probably from the ferry which operated across the Wye at this point until just after the First World War. The woods through which the walk has frequently passed are owned by the Forestry Commission and are known as Tintern Forest.

FURTHER READING:	Useful notes on industrial remains of the Tintern area in 'An Industrial Tour of the Wye Valley and Forest of Dean', by H.W. Parr (W. London Industrial Archaeological Society, 1980) obtainable at the Tintern Railway Station Information Centre.

WALK 3 THE SEVERN WOODFORD–LITTLE AVON RIVER–WHITCLIFF PARK–STONE–WOODFORD

DESCRIPTION:	A walk, along a peaceful river, visiting the oldest inhabited castle in the country, passing through fields and bridlepaths to an attractive village.
MAPS:	OS 1:50,000 Sheet 162 (Gloucester and Forest of Dean). OS 1:25,000 ST 69/79 (Dursley and Wotton-under-Edge).
DISTANCE:	6 miles or 7½ miles including visit to Berkeley Castle.
TERRAIN:	Flat apart from a steep climb into the deer park.
FOOD AND DRINK:	Pubs at Stone and Ham.
TRANSPORT:	Gloucester/Berkeley bus from Bristol – regular. Bus stops right by start of the walk.
START AND FINISH:	Woodford, on A38, ½ mile beyond Stone Church, opposite Damery turning, signposted to Berkeley.

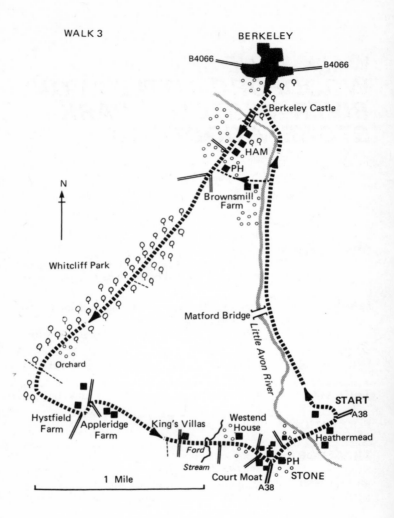

WALK 3

BERKELEY

B4066

B4066

Berkeley Castle

HAM

PH

Brownsmill
Farm

N

Whitcliff Park

Matford Bridge

Little Avon River

Orchard

START

A38

Hystfield
Farm

Appleridge
Farm

King's Villas

Westend
House

Heathermead

Ford

Court Moat

PH

STONE

Stream

A38

1 Mile

There is ample parking on the minor road opposite the start of the walk, where the road has been realigned, leaving a parallel stretch at the signpost to Damery and Huntingford.

Pass the cottages and take the hunting gate on the right. Follow the stony track forward, then bearing right along the hedge, and where the hedge turns away from you go forward until you can see over the brow of the field a stile in front of a horse jump, just down to the left. Climb this stile and follow the bank of the **Little Avon River.** You will see Berkeley Castle ahead of you. In the summer the flowers and butterflies are numerous along this stretch, and at any season you will probably put up a mallard from a hidden haunt. The path goes through nine fields in all, on its way to Berkeley, and is very easy to follow. As you near the castle you will come close to a farm on your left, with a footbridge leading to it. *If you do not wish to visit Berkeley and want to shorten the walk, go over this footbridge, pass the farm and continue straight along the road to a grassy triangle at Ham. At the road ahead the main route will join in from your right. There is an inn just along to your right.*

For Berkeley, keep going along the river, and through the gate ahead by the footbridge. Continue to another stile and gate, and in the last field before the castle follow the well-trodden path away from the river, diagonally right. You will see fencing and a gate and stile to the road, very near to the castle. Turn right at the road, and right again for the castle if you wish to visit it.

Berkeley Castle is the oldest inhabited castle in the country and one family has lived there for 700 years. It is famous as the place where Edward II met his death. The little town of Berkeley is worth exploring.

Return to the stile where you emerged on to the road, and continue along the road, away from the castle. You will soon pass the **kennels of the Berkeley Hunt,** and, passing an inn, arrive at the little village green at **Ham.** The shorter walk joins here.

Just past the green you will come to a road junction. Go through the field gate in the angle of the two roads, and make for a ladder stile over the wall into **Whitcliff Park,** just to the right of the house. Follow the track, which bears right at the lodge gate and goes up on to the ridge. You now follow this ridge for the whole length of the park. On a clear day there are magnificent views over the Severn and the Cotswolds, with the clump of trees on May Hill and the monuments at North Nibley and Hawkesbury Upton showing up clearly. You will also have a good view of Berkeley Power Station.

Follow along the line of trees; some of them are chestnuts and are a lovely sight in the spring. The deer are usually down to the right, but they may occasionally come near to the path. Pass through the swing gate in the deer fence and continue ahead to the wall at the end of the park. Climb another ladder stile, by a house. The path now continues to the left, keeping close to the wall, but this is sometimes very muddy and you may have to pick your way by the best route, but return to the wall and where it ends go down the steep path through the bushes, slightly to your left, and join a crossing track. Turn right and in a few yards you will find a stile hidden in the left-hand hedge. Climb it and walk the length of the field with the hedge on your right, to emerge via a gate on to the road. A few yards to your right you will find a stile in the opposite hedge. Cross the field, keeping the farm just to your right, to another stile in the opposite hedge, near the barn. Go forward across the next field, keeping fairly near the right-hand hedge and making for the left of the second large, oak tree from the right-hand corner. There is a stile at this tree. Climb it and cross the next field straight ahead, making for the corner near the cattle trough. You will see a stile in the hedge right ahead of you. Do not cross this: the path goes to the right over a stile and hidden footbridge about 30 yards before the facing hedge. This brings you to a green lane, which you follow left to the road.

Almost opposite you will see another signposted bridleway. Follow this peaceful path, which is loud with bird song in the spring, until it turns left and joins a road. Turn right here and you will reach the village green at **Stone.** The church is just to your left and there is an inn opposite for refreshment. After exploring the village, turn left along the A38 and cross it where a road joins in left, by a guest house. You will find a footpath going down parallel to the road. This is a much more pleasant route than just returning along the A38, and it gives an opportunity to cross the Little Avon River again and to see another of its mills, converted to a house, on your right. The road ahead leads uphill to the start of the walk.

WALK 4 THE SEVERN
FRAMPTON-ON-SEVERN–
SAUL–FRETHERNE–
FRAMPTON-ON-SEVERN

DESCRIPTION:	A waterside walk – alongside lake, canal and river. Frampton-on-Severn has beautiful timbered houses, one of the largest village greens in the country, and a handsome Georgian house (Frampton Court). Good walk for birdwatchers.
MAPS:	OS 1:50,000 Sheet 162 (Gloucester and Forest of Dean). OS 1:25,000 SO 70 (1st Series).
DISTANCE:	9 miles.
TERRAIN:	Very flat and easy.
FOOD AND DRINK:	At Frampton.
TRANSPORT:	No direct bus from Bristol. Private services operate locally.
START AND FINISH:	On the B4071 ¾ mile from A38.

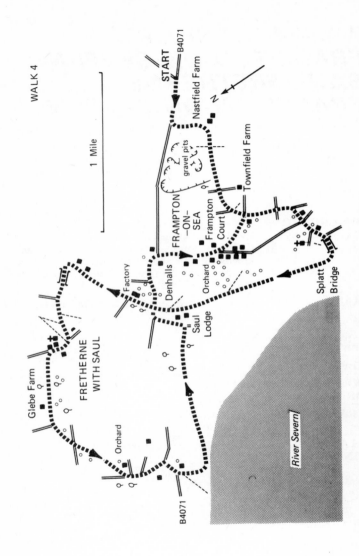

WALK 4

START

B4071

Nastfield Farm

N

1 Mile

gravel pits

Townfield Farm

FRAMPTON
–ON–
SEA

Frampton
Court

Factory

Denhalls

Orchard

Saul
Lodge

FRETHERNE
WITH SAUL

Glebe Farm

Orchard

Splatt
Bridge

B4071

River Severn

If coming by car there is space for two or three on the verge of the first turning right after leaving A38.

Continue on down the B4071 towards Frampton, and take the track on the left towards **Nastfield Farm.** The track starts three quarters of a mile from the A38. Before reaching the farm buildings, take a wide track on the right. Keep straight along this track, and you will come to the old gravel pits on your right, half hidden behind the bushes.

There are plenty of gaps to see through, however, and you will find that in late summer the beautiful yellow of the water lilies covers almost the whole surface of one of the lakes. You will hear the call of mallard everywhere, and often the large flocks of Canada and greylag geese will take off and fly overhead with their loud honking sound. Cormorants may be seen, often resting in the trees on the islands in the big lake which you will soon come to on your right. There are many species of duck, particularly in winter, and numerous gulls. If you are very lucky you will see the brilliant flash of blue as a kingfisher darts by, but even if you do not see it you may hear its sharp note.

As the track bends round to the left, to the buildings, do not follow it but go through a squeeze stile ahead, into the field. Walk along the edge of the lake; then go ahead through another stile into the next field. Here turn half left and make for the headquarters of the **Sailing Club,** which looks like a barn. It has been very well converted to fit in with the surroundings. Climb the stile, cross the track and climb two more stiles into the field. Turn left to the field boundary and walk along this until you join a footpath and pass another small lake. Red-crested pochard are sometimes to be seen here. Continue ahead to the road, cross straight over and go along the lane behind the houses. A stile on your right brings you into another lane and out on to the main village street in **Frampton-on-Severn.** Take the road almost opposite, passing a lovely old barn on your right. A visit to the church will prove worthwhile, for it has a lovely Norman font. Return to follow the lane to **Splatt Bridge,** over the Gloucester and Sharpness canal.

After crossing the bridge turn right along the towpath, walking the length of the village to the road bridge. Cross over and continue straight ahead along the towpath to the next bridge, passing **Cadbury's factory** on your right. Leave the canal and turn left along the lane to **Saul church;** turn right at the T-junction, then first left. At the next junction, go straight ahead through the gate and cross the field, bearing slightly left and making for a stile to the right of two large oak trees. Climb the stile, cross the road and the stile opposite, and walk along the field with the fence on your left. There is a house nearby on your right. Cross the stile at the end of the field, and then make for a stile just to the right of the farm. This leads to a gate ahead on to the road, where turn left to **Fretherne church.**

Fretherne is one of the Severn's delightul villages and looks up to Barrow hill, from which can be seen miles of river and about 40 churches. The church here is 19th century and lavishly decorated.

Turn right for about two hundred yards. Then, at the brick cottage, take the signposted path through the gate on the left. Cross the field, bearing slightly right to a gate at the far end. Go through the gate and cross the next field, following the left hedge. You will find a stile in this, just before the river bank is reached. Climb the stile and follow along the river bank for three quarters of a mile. *This would be a peaceful spot to picnic or to watch birds, for the view out across the wide expanse of the Severn to the Forest shore opposite is quite remarkable.*

Cross the stream by climbing the gates over the sluice, turn inland and cross the stile to your right. The path goes straight ahead to a gate, just to the left of the Water Board installation, through the gate, and straight ahead to another. Go through the gate, not the stile to its left, into a green track, and follow this straight ahead over two stiles. The latter section may be overgrown in summer but it is passable, and you will see a massive badger set on the path. Turn left to follow a track back to the road, where turn right and cross the canal bridge which you crossed previously. Keep straight ahead for a quarter of a mile and you will find on your right the village green of Frampton-on-Severn.

Its old-fashioned cottages and houses look across to the green, reputed to be one of the biggest in the country. It was once a marsh and was reclaimed by the builder of Frampton Court, the beautiful Georgian house nearby. There are ponds and a grove of chestnut trees on the green, and it is well worth spending some time looking at the village.

About half a mile along from the end of the green where you joined it, and just before reaching houses facing you on the left, is a track on the left which will take you back to the **Sailing Club.** Opposite the clubhouse, climb the stile on your left, go half-right to the stile and retrace your steps alongside the lake on your left, through the squeeze stile and forward along the track until you reach the crossing track just before **Nastfield Farm.** Turn left along this track to reach the road; then turn right back to your car or bus.

WALK 5 THE COTSWOLDS
COALEY PEAK–ULEY–OWLPEN–NYMPSFIELD–COALEY PEAK

DESCRIPTION:	A walk for a clear day to appreciate the delightful views over the Severn to the Black Mountains. Uley is a delightful Cotswold village and Owlpen with its Elizabethan manor house and church is a hidden gem.
MAPS:	OS 1:50,000 sheet 162 (Gloucester and Forest of Dean). OS 1:25,000 ST 69/79 (Dursley and Wotton-under-Edge). SO 70 (1st Series).
DISTANCE:	8 miles.
TERRAIN:	Hilly – 2 fairly steep descents and ascents.
FOOD AND DRINK:	At Nympsfield and Uley.
TRANSPORT:	Buses to Dursley then infrequently on to Coaley Peak (Stroud service).
START AND FINISH:	Picnic site and car park at the top of Frocester Hill, on Uley–Stroud road.

WALK 5

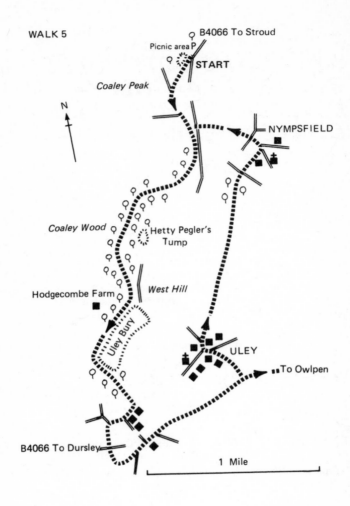

B4066 To Stroud
Picnic area P
START
Coaley Peak
N
NYMPSFIELD
Coaley Wood
Hetty Pegler's Tump
West Hill
Hodgecombe Farm
Uley Bury
ULEY
To Owlpen
B4066 To Dursley
1 Mile

36

Both *Uley* and *Nympsfield* are attractive villages, with ruins. Hetty Pegler's Tump *is only a mile or so from Coaley Peak towards Uley. It is a neolithic long barrow where it is thought some 28 people were buried in a roofed chamber. Uley is full of houses of architectural distinction, built by clothiers. Broadcloth and Spanish cloth were made here and Uley blues were famous.*

Uley Bury, 800 feet high, is one of the finest prehistoric camps in Gloucestershire. A great tribal centre where two or three thousand people take refuge, it had two banks and ditches enclosing 30 acres. Roman coins and pottery have been found, but it pre-dates the Romans.

The walk starts at the picnic site and car park at the top of **Frocester Hill,** on the road from Uley to Stroud.

There is an excavated long barrow at the picnic site, after which go through the gate into the paddock and continue along the fence, with a marvellous view out over the Severn to the hills beyond. Climb the stile at the end and turn right to the topograph. This will indicate to you the various points to be seen from this spot on a clear day, and the distances to the points of interest. Returning from the topograph – do not go back over the stile into the paddock which you have just climbed but bear right and follow the waymarked path into the quarry. This is a sheltered spot and very good for wild flowers and butterflies in summer. The path continues through the quarry and by way of steps comes out on to the road near the top of **Frocester Hill.**

Cross over and walk up to the road junction, bear right, and then in only a few yards take the signposted bridleway down through the wood on your right. This does tend to be muddy in parts during wet weather. The official route is waymarked, as it is part of **Cotswold Way,** but there are small paths to avoid the worst of the mud if it is bad. At the bottom of the hill there is a junction of ways and a cottage in front of you. Turn left before the cottage, then very shortly left again, up into the wood, still following the Cotswold Way. *This wood is delightful in bluebell time, as you can look down from the path on to a sea of misty blue. The colours in autumn are also beautiful.* The path will lead you past a quarry face, shortly before climbing to a junction of paths at the roadside. Follow the bridleway to your right, alongside the road, at the top going to the right over a cattle grid. You are now on the ramparts of **Uley Bury,** an Iron Age hill fort and one of the best in the county. *Again the views are wide and it is well worth lingering to enjoy the fresh air amid such delightful surroundings.*

Follow round two sides of the camp, and just after the next cattle grid look for a path going off downhill to your right. Follow this through the wood, ignoring paths on the right. This section is steep and can be slippery in wet weather. At the bottom of the wood go over the stile and walk down the right-hand side of the field to the bottom right-hand corner. Climb the stile to your right and keep straight ahead when reaching the road at **Whitecourt.** *There are interesting* *glimpses of weavers' cottages in this road.* At the junction by the chapel keep right. The road bends sharp right by a nursery. Take the track on the left immediately after the nursery wall, and follow it for 250 yards to a stile on your left, soon after a house on the right. Climb the stile and cross straight ahead to another stile, which will bring you to the **Uley–Dursley** road, almost opposite a house.

Cross straight over and climb the stile to the left of the house; then go ahead down the field to a stile and footbridge over the **River Ewelme.** Then cross diagonally left uphill to go through a gate just before the house. Bear right to the lane; then walk along this to the road junction. Bear left; then at the T-junction ahead turn right and go uphill for 100 yards to a path on your left by **Stouts Hill Cottage,** signposted to Owlpen. Follow this across a track and then past a beech hedge. There is a beautifully converted mill to your left. Climb the stile ahead and pass the mill pond. Keep along the left hedge, parallel with the stream, and climb a stile in the opposite hedge. Then cross the next field, bearing slightly right. Climb the stile and go downhill to a footbridge over a tiny stream, then straight along the left-hand hedge. Go ahead through another gate, and you will pass another converted mill building. Still following the stream, continue through this peaceful valley and over another stile. In the next field you will find a substantial footbridge on your left, at the beginning of a wood. This wood is growing in the remains of the reservoir which stored the water to power the mill you have just passed. You can still see the grassy dam.

To visit Owlpen, continue straight ahead along the stream you have been following, to cross another stile and another field and emerge on to the tiny road via another stile. *If you wish to shorten the walk, re-join the directions at the footbridge mentioned above. At the road you will see the manor house with its lovely gardens and the church behind it. You may visit the church, but the manor is open only by prior arrangement. If you would like a better view of the manor, however, there is a footpath in the field in front of it, straight opposite where you joined the road. It goes along the left-hand fence.*

At the stile where you joined the road, retrace your steps through one field and into the second, where the footbridge will now be on your right. From here you can look up to the church, and to Uley Bury towering above it. You can see your path ahead, crossing the first field diagonally left, then over a stile and forward up the hill to the right-hand one of two telegraph poles, then to a very tall tree and over a stile to bring you to a path between gardens. Follow this round to left and right, and you will come out on the village green. There is refreshment here if needed, and the church is almost opposite. There are some very attractive houses to be seen around the green.

Follow the main road up to your right for a few yards, and where it turns sharp left carry on straight ahead along a lane towards

Mutterall Farm. Take a footpath on the left immediately beyond the first cottage on your left, climb a stile and go straight forward over an electric fence and continue ahead to a gate and stile. Cross the next field in the same direction; then in the third field bear half right to find a footbridge over the stream. Now continue up the valley in the same direction as before, following the stream on your left, and crossing a stile. Continue until you see a stile into a wood on your left. Go over this and follow the main path to the right, steeply up to the head of the valley. It emerges on to a road by a house. Cross straight over and walk down the left-hand hedge of the field, to leave by a stone stile to the left of a barn. Another stile will bring you to the road in Nympsfield village.

Turn left, pass the inn. The church is to your right if you wish to visit it and take the next turning left. Just after the houses go over a stile on your right and walk along the field with the hedge on your right. Then at the end continue ahead with the hedge on your left. Go straight ahead and you will reach the road by way of a stile. You are almost opposite the picnic site.

WALK 6 THE COTSWOLDS
PAINSWICK–PITCHCOMBE–HARESFIELD BEACON–EDGE COMMON–PAINSWICK

DESCRIPTION:	Beautiful Cotswold scenery and buildings are seen on this walk. Dramatic views from Haresfield Beacon contrast with the peace of the Painswick stream and the woodland stretches.
MAPS:	OS 1:50,000 sheet 162 (Gloucester and Forest Dean). OS 1:25,000 SO 80 (1st Series).
DISTANCE:	12 miles.
TERRAIN:	Some steep climbing and descending woodland tracks; can be very muddy in wet weather.
FOOD AND DRINK:	At Painswick and Edge Common.
TRANSPORT:	Buses from Gloucester, Stroud and Cheltenham, which can all be reached by train from Bristol.
START:	Painswick.
FINISH:	Painswick.

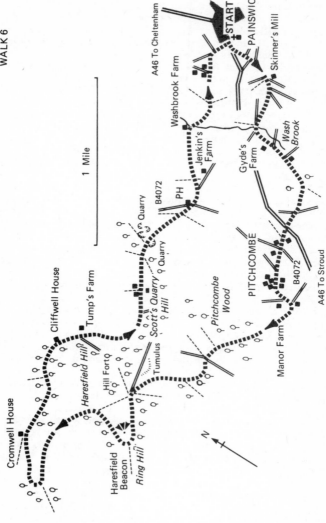

Washbrook Farm

A46 To Cheltenham

START

PAINSWICK

Skinner's Mill

1 Mile

Jenkin's Farm

Wash Brook

Gyde's Farm

B4072

PH

Quarry

Quarry

Quarry

Scott's Quarry

Hill

PITCHCOMBE

Cliffwell House

Tump's Farm

Haresfield Hill

Hill Fort

Tumulus

Pitchcombe Wood

B4072

A46 To Stroud

Manor Farm

Cromwell House

Haresfield Beacon

Ring Hill

N

The walk starts at the car park in **Stamages Lane,** just a few hundred yards down the A46 from Painswick church.

Go down the lane, which becomes **Stepping Stones Lane** at the crossroads, and into the valley bottom. Opposite the entrance to **Skinners Mill,** now a farm, is a stile on the bank of the Painswick stream. Cross it and continue ahead along the bank through the meadows, a bank rich with bird song in the spring and pink with balsam in the summer. You will see a lovely house to your right, its garden sloping down to the river. Then cross a stile and the weir and emerge on to a track at the side of **King's Mill House.** What a wonderful sight, as you turn left and see its full beauty! *There has been a mill on this spot since 1495, and water power was still being used to turn its wheels at the beginning of this century.* The long weavers' windows on the upper storeys have been retained.

Continue on the track, crossing the stream again and making for the next building. This is called **Sheephouse,** and although the path goes straight ahead through the buildings, a few paces to the left will reveal the courtyard of this beautiful building. The gable end facing it contains about 100 holes for doves. Return to the track along which you have just walked, and go straight ahead through the buildings, with the delightful **Dovecote Cottage** on your right. This leads to a wooden swing gate and straight ahead to a stile. Glancing back one can see the spire of Painswick church, and ahead on the right you will notice Pitchcombe church high on the hillside. After climbing the stile, go downhill to your left on a rutted track to cross the valley and climb out of it to a stile in the extreme right-hand corner of the fence opposite, by a tall ash tree. After the stile, aim for an oak tree half right, and pass near to an old barn on stone pillars. As you go over the brow of the hill you will be confronted by a beautiful scene.

Weavers Mill *ahead of you is a real gem of Cotswold architecture and its gardens beautiful at any time of the year. Willows line the mill stream, the sluice gate for which is retained, and across the lawn you can see a lake.*

Climb the stile between the two houses and go down the steps to the road. As you turn right you will see that the old machinery has been beautifully preserved. There are cider presses in the garden. The colourful bank of heather borders a lake, on which you can see water birds – if they are not sunning themselves on the lawn. Just opposite the lake take the stile into the field, and make for the electricity pole. As you climb you can look back over this delightful settlement, before going straight ahead to a wooden stile at the side of a gate, leading on to the A46.

Cross the road and go left to a stile a few yards away. Go steeply up the field; then bear left to make for the red-roofed house in the corner. Here a stile will bring you on to a footpath – lovely for snowdrops in early spring – and then the track ahead will lead you to the road just below **Pitchcombe** church. Cross over and take the tiny road into the village. *Time has left Pitchcombe strictly alone, and as you continue round its narrow road you will find much to please the eye, from the tiniest of cottages to an elegant frontage with twenty windows, a glimpse of old, gabled houses hidden down a path, and the real gem of the village – the beautifully preserved mill with its large pond. You could spend half an hour just savouring these delights, before climbing steeply up the hill and looking back to appreciate the setting of this quiet village.* Painswick is still visible, too, with its majestic spire.

Continue to the crossroads and take the 'No through road' to the right. Go ahead through the hand gate at the end of the road and climb steeply straight ahead. The views to your left now begin to open out, and you can see Stroud straggling up its steep valleys and the 18th century house, Rodborough Fort, high on top of the common. Selsley Common lies far out beyond, and the nearer church is Whiteshill. Keep straight uphill, over a stile, and as you enter the long field you will see the roof of **Stoneridge Farm** on the skyline. Make for this, and just in front of it go over a stile at the side of a gate to walk up a narrow pathway on to the road. Cross it and take the Randwick turning opposite.

In only about 75 yards climb the stile on your right, just before the wood. Walk along the edge of the wood, noting the unusual stone stiles into it. At the third of these, when there are bushes just in front of you, go through into the wood and turn right on the well worn path. This leads you to a squeeze stile into a car park and out through another one to cross the field straight ahead to the topograph on the farthest promontory.

This shows you what you should be able to see across the Severn on a clear day, if it is not actually clear enough to see it. The view over the river to the Forest of Dean and the hills beyond it is truly magnificent. Continue round the top of the scarp, following the waymarks. The next objective, **Ring Hill,** is clearly seen. You will come to some steps on your right. Go up these to the road, turn left, and take the stony track out to the trig point on **Haresfield Beacon.** You are on the site of a hill fort. *This spot is the haunt of kestrels, and you will see them hanging almost effortlessly in the wind.* Continue on round the edge of the hill, dropping to reach the farm buldings, still following the waymarks. Cross a stile and emerge on to the road.

Turn left for a few yards and take the bridleway on the opposite side of the road. You will have noticed the city of Gloucester lying in the vale, its cathedral standing out clearly. You will continue to see it, and the nearer Robins Wood Hill, from this bridleway. At a right-hand bend you will come to the stone commemorating the siege of Gloucester in 1643. Further down you will find a building housing an old well. Cross the road and take the lane almost opposite, signposted to **Tumps Farm.** At the entrance to the farm take the gate on the right, and, keeping the farm buildings close on your left, follow round the field to an iron gate. Cross the next field to a stile, keeping round the bottom of the steep slope. The stile is in the point of the hedge, just to the right of a group of large trees. Go ahead to the corner of a hedge in front of you, and through the gap, to continue with the hedge on your right, to a stile. Go straight ahead, with a small farmhouse on your left, to a gate on to the track. Keep straight along this track until it becomes metalled and joins the road proper through two stone gateposts.

Turn right and go along the track, keeping left at the cottage facing you, and in a few yards you will come to a tiny path up the hill on your left, with a stile on your right and a house immediately below it. Go steeply up the hillside to the road, cross straight over and go down the steps into a quarry. Climb out opposite, and look to the right for a waymarked post. Follow the waymarks over the common to emerge on to the road at the **'Edgemoor' Inn.** Go down the lane right opposite, and just before the farm go through the squeeze stile on your left. Make for the next stile in the fence on the right, then down the field to some steps in the bottom right-hand corner. Cross the stream and go to the right up through the trees, crossing a stile into a field. Go ahead to a stile on the left which leads to a track into the yard of Washbrook Farm.

Keep all the buildings on your right until you reach the house; then turn right and pass close by it. Notice how much it has been altered since it was built in the 17th century; it has been a cloth and a corn mill. Go up past the paddock to a stile at the edge of the wood. Climb the stile, keep left and follow the hedge for about two hundred yards. Now cross the field towards a stile, but do not climb this; carry on to another right in the corner of the field. Cross this and go up the slope towards a waymarked telegraph pole, where turn right to take the path alongside the garden of the nearest house. At the squeeze stile at the end, turn sharp right along another path and over a stile into a field and thence on to the road. Turn right and you will see ahead of you the church gatehouse, which is made partly from old timbers of the belfry and has bargeboards carved with bells. Before you reach this, however, there are more Cotswold houses to enjoy. When you have seen sufficient of the 15th century church, with its famous yew trees, and the delightful houses around, the car park is just down the hill.

WALK 7 THE COTSWOLDS
OLD SODBURY–LITTLE SODBURY–HORTON–TORMARTON–OLD SODBURY

DESCRIPTION:	A scenic walk ascending the Cotswold edge to about 600 feet. It takes in parkland, unspoiled villages, and can be extended to see Horton Court and Dodington House.
MAPS:	OS 1:50,000 Sheet 172 (Bristol and Bath). OS 1:25,000 ST 77 (1st Series).
DISTANCE:	10 miles.
TERRAIN:	Some steep climbing is involved to reach hilltop forts.
FOOD AND DRINK:	Pubs at Old Sodbury and Tormarton.
TRANSPORT:	Bus: Bristol–Old Sodbury. Regular to Chipping Sodbury and occasional thereafter.
START AND FINISH:	'Dog' Inn, Old Sodbury.

WALK 7

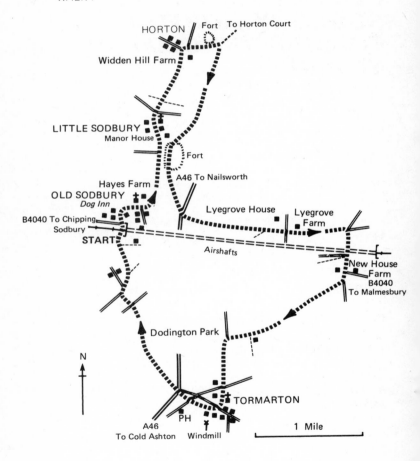

HORTON   Fort   To Horton Court

Widden Hill Farm

LITTLE SODBURY
Manor House

Fort

A46 To Nailsworth

Hayes Farm

OLD SODBURY
Dog Inn

B4040 To Chipping
Sodbury

START

Lyegrove House   Lyegrove
Farm

Airshafts

New House
Farm
B4040
To Malmesbury

Dodington Park

N

TORMARTON

A46
To Cold Ashton

PH

Windmill

1 Mile

46

Start at the 'Dog' Inn at Old Sodbury. There are parking places in quiet roads nearby. *Old Sodbury is delightful for its hilly ways, its fine views, and the treasures in the ancient church perched high on a hill. Man has looked out on to the view for 800 years from its churchyard, and for far longer from the hill behind the churches of Old and Little Sodbury, on which is a camp of about 12 acres. Built by ancient Britons and fortified by the Romans, it was one of the biggest camps in England and was used in later years by King Edward as a resting place when he set out for the battle of Tewkesbury.* Cross the main road and enter Cotswold Lane, but do not go along the lane. Instead, look for a stone public footpath sign set in the ground on your left, and go through the yard behind it, leaving by way of a gate on the right at the far end. Cross the field and climb the stile slightly to the right. Then turn sharp right, up the steep grassy slope, to Old Sodbury church. The path goes through the churchyard and out to the road, but the church is a must to those interested.

It is eight hundred years old and contains among many other things a life-sized carving of a man, in oak, and another figure of a knight, in stone. From the churchyard there are views of the tree-clad Cotswold slopes, the tower of Chipping Sodbury church rising among the houses, and the hills of Gwent beyond the Severn.

On leaving the churchyard, walk a few paces to the right along the road. Then take the footpath on the left, immediately before the school. The path is well trodden and continues along the bottom of the slope, through beautiful trees, until at a gate it joins a green lane. Turn left down this lane to the road, by a waterworks installation. Turn right at the road, and in a few minutes you will pass on your right the gabled manor house of Little Sodbury, dating from the 15th century. *It was the home at one time of William Tyndale, who translated the New Testament, and who is commemorated by the monument at North Nibley which you will see on this walk if the weather is clear. The ruins of the mediaeval church are high on a bank by the manor house, and stones from it were used to build the present church, which you will come to further along the road. Notice the beautiful Cotswold style house on your left before this, though.* At the church, the only one in England dedicated to St. Adeline, turn right for a very short distance to the footpath sign on your left at the far side of the house. This will take you right past the side of the house to a stile on your right into a field. Follow the left-hand hedge through the fields until you reach the reservoir in the valley bottom. This is a peaceful spot and you may be lucky enough to see little grebe and coot swimming amongst the reeds. Look up to the skyline, where you will see a hunt gate—do not follow the track which goes in the direction of the large grey house on the hilltop to your right. Climb steeply up the grassy slope through the gate and forward across the field, where the path emerges just to the right of the left-hand house. It is marked by posts as the field is often in crop. Go through the gate and forward to the road, opposite **Post Cottage,** in the village of **Horton.** Turn right for a few yards to the road junction, then turn left for another few yards.

If you wish to extend the walk to see Horton Court and church, continue along this road for just over half a mile, but return to this spot. Horton Court belongs to the National Trust. It has a Norman wing alongside the perpendicular church, and in the garden a late Gothic ambulatory.

At the footpath sign just past the school, go into the field and walk up the right-hand boundary for about thirty yards. Go through an iron field gate and walk diagonally left uphill. As you pass under the ramparts of the hill fort you will see the large grey stone house which you noticed from the reservoir below, now on your right. Keep well to the left of this and continue along the left-hand boundary of the field in the direction of the new bungalow. Just before reaching its grounds, cross the fence to your left and pass the wooden stable to climb a stile in the right-hand fence just beyond. Climb the rampart of this old British camp and continue straight ahead to the footpath sign at the road, keeping the new bungalow to your right. The camp is delightful to those who love distant views from lonely places and to have about them a scene of tranquillity still much as it was in Norman times. Turn right at the road and follow it to the junction. Cross over and walk down the wide grassy verge ahead. Ignore the turning downhill to Horton. To shorten the walk, cutting out the camp, continue straight up the road out of Horton and do not turn left at the school. You will rejoin the main route at this point.

Continue along the road singposted to Little Sodbury, and follow it to the T-junction at the end. There is a grassy verge to walk on. There are marvellous views all the way, and you will get a glimpse of the reservoir far below. At the road junction go straight forward over a stile, cross the field in a straight line and go over another stile. In this field make for the right-hand end of the farm buildings. There is a path at the side of the greenhouse, followed by a gate on the right. Go through and turn left to follow the buildings round. Do not try to climb the wire fence ahead of you – there is a gate through it a few more yards on. Go through the gate and turn right in a few yards to enter the camp. This is **Sodbury camp,** *an area of about twelve acres, built by ancient Britons and fortified by the Romans. It is one of the biggest camps in England.*

Cross the camp by the well-worn path and make for the tall trees ahead. Go through the gate by the trees and walk diagonally left across the field to a gap in the opposite wall, by a cattle trough, making for the buildings, not the nearby filling station. Go through the next field to the footpath sign in the left-hand corner of the opposite wall, and emerge on to the **A46,** just before the houses.

Cross the A46 carefully and take the bridle-way across the fields, noting the air shafts for the railway tunnel on your right. In the third field make for a hand gate to your left. Then follow the right-hand wall along to another hand gate, and enter a green lane. At the end continue along the left-hand wall, and where it bends sharply to the left, continue straight across the large field to a hand gate at the far side. Go ahead through the line of trees, passing the farm, to the end of a rough track, and a bridle-way signpost by the road.

Turn right along the road, pass a grassy triangle with a clump of trees, ignore the turning to the right, and continue ahead to the farm you will see in front of you on the right-hand side of the road. Just past this, take a track to the right, which shortly bears left. It is a very pleasant track, with good views back to Badminton House. Where the track ends, carry straight on through field gates, keeping the little wood to your left, and you will pick up the track again, to emerge on to a road. Turn left and you will shortly come to Tormarton. Cross over at the crossroads and continue to the church. *This is Norman, and the west porch is unusual in that it has three doorways, two of which are filled in.*

Take the path over the stone stile opposite the church, and go half left to a telegraph pole near a barn, where a stile will bring you to the road. Turn left along the village street for about a hundred yards, to the path on the right by the **Old Schoolhouse.** You may wish to explore the village further, as it is very attractive, but return to this point. Keep to the right-hand side of the field, cross a stile, a minor road, the field ahead and another minor road. There are refreshments available at the inn just to your left here. Cross straight ahead across one more field, to the A46. Cross this and climb the stile opposite. Go ahead, then shortly right, to cross the **River Frome** just below its source, by a footbridge and stile at a large tree. You are now in **Dodington Park.** Go ahead, making towards the trees on your right, and walk along the field by the right-hand boundary to reach a gate at the far end. Go through the gate and head for a prominent group of trees (mostly beech) on the hillside opposite. As you descend steeply you will find a stile in the fence below you, leading to another one and then to a small stone bridge. Cross this and go ahead to a gate on the track which leads, left, to Dodington House and church. Cross the track and go forward across the grass to a gate to the road. Turn right, and pass the road junction and carry on uphill to the end of the cottages. Turn left through a gate at the side of the last cottage. Go straight forward through a gateway then over a stile opposite, then left to a gate in the far corner of the field and finally a gate to the road ahead.

You will notice Old Sodbury church ahead as you cross these fields. Turn right on the road and you will reach the **'Dog' Inn** in less than half a mile.

WALK 8 BRISTOL
CLIFTON–ASHTON PARK–
ABBOTS POOL–LEIGH
WOODS–CLIFTON

DESCRIPTION:	A scenic walk very close to Bristol and ideal for a summer evening. It takes in the spectacular Avon Gorge, quiet field paths and parkland, and affords excellent views across Avon and Severn.
MAPS:	OS 1:50,000 Sheet 172 (Bristol and Bath). OS 1:25,000 ST 47/67 (Portishead and Bristol (West)).
DISTANCE:	5 miles (Suspension bridge back to Suspension bridge).
TERRAIN:	Very easy paths, tracks and quiet roads with very little climbing.
FOOD AND DRINK:	At the 'George', Abbots Leigh, and near Clifton Green.
TRANSPORT:	Frequent buses to Clifton Green.
START AND FINISH:	Clifton Suspension Bridge.

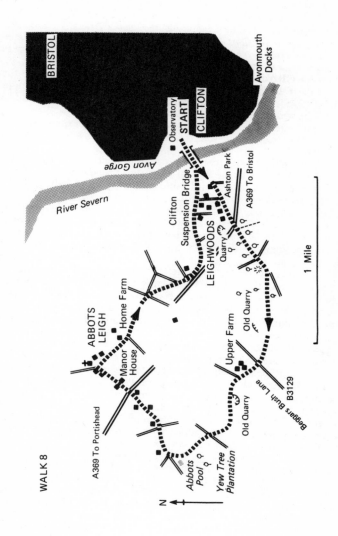

WALK 8

BRISTOL

Avon Gorge

River Severn

Observatory ■
START
CLIFTON

Avonmouth Docks

Clifton
Suspension Bridge

LEIGHWOODS

Ashton Park

A369 To Bristol

Quarry

ABBOTS
LEIGH

Home Farm

Manor
House

Upper Farm

Old Quarry

Beggars Bush Lane

B3129

A369 To Portishead

Abbots
Pool

Yew Tree
Plantation

Old Quarry

N

1 Mile

51

In 1829 Brunel entered a competition for the design of a bridge to span the Avon Gorge, but Thomas Telford, the judge, rejected his design because he thought the spans were too great, and produced his own design. Four judges were then appointed and they chose Brunel's plans, thus beginning his connections with Bristol and the West country. Work on the bridge started in 1831 but lack of money led to its abandonment in 1854 and Brunel died before the bridge was finished in 1864.

Start at **Clifton Suspension Bridge.** Sheer below you are the bare cliffs of the Clifton side, and opposite the thickly wooded slopes of Leigh Woods – a remarkable contrast of scenery for two banks of a river. The water is about 250 feet below you as you cross. There is a small toll for pedestrians, but it is well worth it just for the view. The stone pillars from which the bridge is suspended are particularly attractive.

On leaving the bridge, continue straight on along **Bridge Road,** until the junction with the Bristol–Portishead road is reached in just under half a mile. Cross carefully and enter the gate of **Ashton Park** ahead. *Ashton Park is a delightful deer park, which has been donated to the citizens of Bristol for their recreation, and is well used and obviously much appreciated.* Continue along the tree-lined track until another track joins it on the right; then leave it and skirt round the trees on your right, going up the grassy slope and making for the left-hand edge of a copse ahead, over the brow of the hill. Leaving one of the greens of the golf course to your left, continue straight ahead uphill, and at the top of the rise you will see the red roofs of farm buildings ahead. The gate out of the park is right opposite these buildings, so, using them as a target, leave another small group of trees well to your left and continue ahead to the belt of trees round the perimeter of the park, where you will find an iron gate in the wall. Go through, cross **Beggars Bush Lane** carefully, and turn left for a few yards.

Take the track on the right, signposted to **Upper Farm.** Past the farm continue straight ahead between fences. Good views over the Bristol Channel now begin to appear, and this is a delightful stretch of countryside, where it is difficult to imagine that you are so near a large city. In about half a mile the track crosses a lane, then continues straight ahead to **Abbots Pool,** hidden in the trees, a favourite spot with anglers and picnickers alike. *It is particularly lovely when the rhododendrons are in flower in late spring, but pleasant enough at all times. It was the fish pond for the nearby Priory, which you will pass shortly.* Turn right across the causeway at the far end of the pool, and at the end go left up a well-worn path, to climb the wooded slope. This path emerges shortly on to a road, which you follow ahead past the houses until it bears sharp right, by a house called **Friars Gate.** Take the path straight ahead here, crossing stiles in front of the garden wall, then join the road for a few yards. Look out for a stile on your left, and climb this to walk on a path parallel to the road. You will glimpse the **Manor House** on your right. When the path re-joins the road, go straight ahead and pass the beautiful buildings of the **Priory** before reaching the crossroads. Refreshment is obtainable at the inn here, if desired.

Cross carefully over the main road. There is a light-controlled crossing just to your right. Then continue straight ahead along the road opposite. The varied styles of architecture make this an interesting road to walk along. Just before reaching **Abbots Leigh church,** a magnificent view opens out to your left.

This is one of the best spots from which to see the Avon bridge, carrying the M5 motorway on a graceful curve over the river. Beyond the bridge are Avonmouth docks, the confluence of the Avon and the Severn, and views across to Gwent. The walk continues across a stile on the right, opposite the church and at the far side of the school. Walk down the field to the stile in the right-hand corner of the next hedge. From here go left uphill towards the farm buildings, go through the gate next to the first barn, and ahead through another one into the farmyard. You will meet the road in just a few yards. Turn left, and soon right, through a field gate on to a track. The way ahead is quite clear, and again there are wide views to be seen. Go through two gates, cross a track and go ahead through another gate, into a field. Go diagonally right across this field, making for an iron field gate between the two bungalows. This leads you on to a track and ahead to the road, near the traffic lights.

Turn left and take the second turning on the left – **North Road.** This has some delightful houses and gardens, and it will lead you on a quiet route back to the Suspension bridge, passing very close to the top of the gorge, where a house built in the style of a Swiss chalet must have one of the best views in Bristol. At the end of North Road you will come back to **Bridge Road,** and turn left to re-cross the Suspension bridge back to Clifton.

WALK 9 BATH
COLD ASHTON– LANSDOWN–FREEZING HILL–DOYNTON–COLD ASHTON

DESCRIPTION:	Dramatic changes from secluded valleys to windy hilltops with extensive views and taking in attractive villages, an Elizabethan manor house and a civil war monument.
MAPS:	OS 1:50,000 Sheet 172 (Bristol and Bath). OS 1:25,000 ST 77 (1st Series).
DISTANCE:	10 miles.
TERRAIN:	Three steep descents and ascents.
FOOD AND DRINK:	Pubs at Cold Ashton, Doynton and Pennsylvania.
TRANSPORT:	Marshfield bus from Bristol or Doynton bus from Bristol. Both regular but infrequent.
START AND FINISH:	Cold Ashton church, just off A420 Bristol–Marshfield road, near juction with A46.

WALK 9

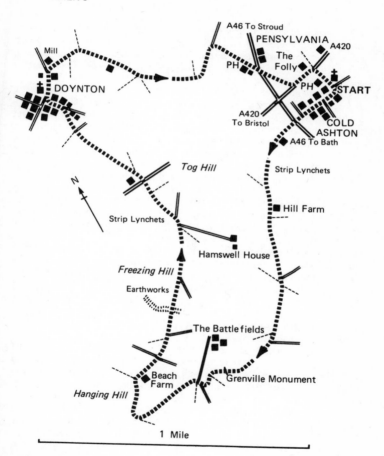

A46 To Stroud

PENSYLVANIA
A420

The Folly

PH

PH

START

Mill

DOYNTON

A420
To Bristol

COLD
ASHTON

A46 To Bath

Strip Lynchets

Tog Hill

Strip Lynchets

Hill Farm

N

Strip Lynchets

Hamswell House

Freezing Hill

Earthworks

The Battlefields

Beach
Farm

Grenville Monument

Hanging Hill

1 Mile

There is public transport to Cold Ashton village, or to Doynton, so you may of course start the walk at either point. If you start at Doynton you will alight from the bus at the church and pick up the route from there. The view from **Cold Ashton** village is a very wide one, and on a windy day you can understand how the village came by its name!

Park near the church and set off along the village street to pass the manor house on your right. *This is an almost perfect example of an Elizabethan Cotswold manor house, set at the head of St. Catherine's valley and commanding magnificent views. It was here that Sir Bevil Grenville was brought when he had been slain in the Battle of Lansdown. You will pass the monument to him later on in the walk. The manor is easily visible from the road.*

Continue along the street to the far end, ignoring a turning to the right, and go forward downhill to cross the A46 and take **Greenways Lane** opposite. This leads down into the valley, passing a farm. At the bottom, where the lane swings left, go forward through a gate and shortly over a stile. Keep the wood on your left and cross ahead to the left-hand gateway in the opposite hedge, making for a barn. Go ahead through the next field to emerge on to the road near a cottage. Turn left over a cattle grid; then walk down the grass parallel to the track, to a hand gate on the left of the next cattle grid. Go through, turn right, cross the stream and the track, and continue ahead uphill. This is a secluded little valley, and grey wagtails are sometimes to be found along the little stream. Go straight up the steep slope, keeping near to the right-hand hedge. Cross a stile into the next field and climb this; then go slightly to the right, to a stile in the opposite hedge. Go over this and keep straight forward, with the hedge on your right, to emerge through a gate on to a green lane. Turn right and go along the lane to a gate at its end. Keep ahead round the top of the steep field until a green track branches off right. Follow this up to the stone steps, to climb the wall and keep ahead along the field boundary. At the end, go through bushes and over a stile, to emerge alongside the **Grenville monument.**

Go ahead to a stile at the road, cross over and walk to your right along the grass verge as far as the track to the **Observer Corps buildings.** Go left along this track, bearing right just in front of the buildings; then take a footpath on your left, skirting close round the buildings. This can be muddy and rather overgrown, but it is excellent for blackberries in the autumn. Go ahead through a gate into the field, where the view really begins to open out. Keep to the top of the field, with the wall on your left, until you reach the **trig point** at the far end, near the wood. This is an excellent spot from which to admire the view, except maybe on a windy day. Turn downhill, still in the same field, and walk diagonally right to join a track at the bottom. This will lead you to a hand gate at the side of a barn and so forward to a gate at the road. Turn right, cross over the

Wick–Bath road, and go ahead for about 300 yards until the road swings sharply to the right.

Go through a gate on your left here, and walk up the left-hand hedge of this very steep field, to cross a stile at the top and continue along the magnificent row of trees, a landmark for miles around. This is **Freezing Hill,** and again it is not difficult to imagine why it is so called. Continue along the field to a gate to the road. Turn left for about half a mile, taking great care as this road can be busy sometimes. Pass the drive to **Hamswell House** on the right. You will have noticed this house high on the hill earlier in the walk. Just past the next house take a track on the left and go through the gate immediately in front of you, not the one round to the left. Keep the hedge on your left and go forward through a gate and straight ahead. The path narrows, but keep straight on to the A420 at **Tog Hill.**

The bridle path used to continue straight under the A420, but the bridge was lost in road widening operations, so cross the road and go ahead to drop into it again on the other side. Proceed down this lane for about a mile – it is very secluded and peaceful but short stretches in the first quarter of a mile can be rather muddy. It becomes surfaced later, and brings you into the charming village of **Doynton.** At the road junction in the centre of the village you may turn left and immediately right to the inn, but the walk continues to the right from the centre of the village, passing the church.

About a quarter of a mile past the church, take the lane on the right, which has a cowshed on the far corner. Walk up to the farm and turn left just before the first of its buildings. Skirt round the back of the buildings and through a gate to reach the back of the house, taking a path diagonally across the field to your left to the right-hand one of two gates. Continue diagonally to the right, to climb a stile into a rather overgrown lane. Cross this and continue up on the outside of the lane, to a field gate. Go ahead up the next field and just before the top go through a gap in the hedge on the right, into the next field. In the top hedge of this you will find a hidden stile. Climb it and bear slightly left but immediately right, to continue up the field with the hedge on your right. The view back now opens out again, and the path continues through a gap ahead and straight across a field to emerge on to the road via a gate.

Cross the road and walk very carefully along to the left until you reach a footpath signpost on your right. This will lead you into the tiny hamlet with the pretentious name of **Pennsylvania,** where there is an inn. Turn right for a few yards and you will see a footpath signpost on your left. Cross diagonally over the field. It is often ploughed, but a path is usually trodden out. Climb the stile and make half left in the direction of the buildings, to the road by the inn. Just past this on your right an iron gate will lead you back into **Cold Ashton churchyard** and through another iron gate on to the street.

WALK 10 AVON VALLEY
BATHAMPTON–CLAVERTON DOWN–MONKTON COMBE–LIMPLEY STOKE–BATHAMPTON

DESCRIPTION:	A varied walk combining the magnificent scenery of steep-sided wooded valleys, picturesque villages and canal towpath; Dundas aqueduct is one of the wonders of the waterway world.
MAPS:	OS 1:50,000 Sheet 172 (Bristol and Bath). OS 1:25,000 ST 66/76 (Bath and Keynsham).
DISTANCE:	11 miles – can be shortened to 7.
TERRAIN:	Two quite steep climbs.
FOOD AND DRINK:	Bathampton has a delightful canalside pub with good food, and there are others at Claverton Down road, Monkton Combe and Limpley Stoke.
TRANSPORT:	Bus from Bath – frequent.
START AND FINISH:	The canal near the 'George' Inn, Bathampton.

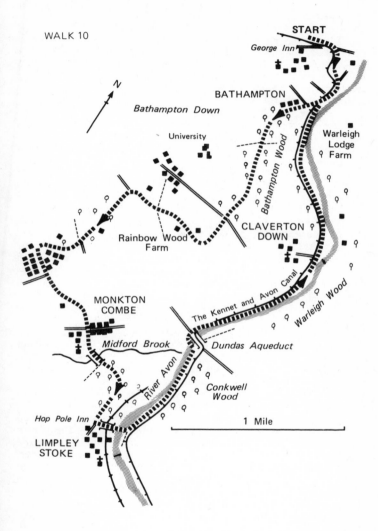

WALK 10

START

George Inn

BATHAMPTON

Bathampton Down

University

Warleigh Lodge Farm

Bathampton Wood

Rainbow Wood Farm

CLAVERTON DOWN

Warleigh Wood

MONKTON COMBE

The Kennet and Avon Canal

Midford Brook

Dundas Aqueduct

River Avon

Conkwell Wood

1 Mile

Hop Pole Inn

LIMPLEY STOKE

The walk begins at the canal near the **'George' Inn** at **Bathampton.** There is ample parking space just further east along the canal: do not cross the bridge from the George but go straight ahead to park opposite the primary school. There is often boating activity taking place here in the summer, when the scene is delightfully colourful. Walk on past the school, on the towpath of the canal, away from Bath. The view down the Limpley Stoke valley soon begins to open out. Continue for about half a mile, until reaching the first bridge. There are often narrow boats moored here, making an attractive scene.

The Kennet and Avon canal was constructed in order to provide a link by water between Bristol and London. John Rennie was the planner and engineer, and the Dundas aqueduct was named after the Chairman of the company. It carries the canal over river and railway, high above the valley, on noble late Georgian arches.

Cross the bridge and go left to a stile in a few yards, which brings you to a grassy track up the hillside. The view gets wider as you climb. You are on the remains of an inclined plane which was constructed to carry the Bath stone down from a quarry to the canal. Unfortunately the bridge which carried it across the road has been lost in road-widening, so soon cross a stile to the road, turn right past the **Dry-Arch Nursery,** cross the road very carefully and take the track going up obliquely on your left, almost opposite. The footpath sign tends to get obscured by overgrowth in the summer. This leads you back to the line of the inclined plane, and as you climb you will see many of the stone blocks to which the rails were once fixed. Follow these blocks right to the top of the hill – you are going to the quarry itself.

Nearly at the top you will notice a stile on your right. Do not climb this but go ahead for only a few yards to the beginning of the main quarry area. Turn left after the very first bushes and follow the most obvious track. You will come into grassy clearings rich in wild flowers, then through bushes again, and you will eventually pass two large rock outcrops. This brings you to a grassy promontory, from which there is an extensive view right out over the valley to the Wiltshire Downs beyond. Turn your back on the view and climb up the bank in front of you, to bring you in a few yards on to the edge of the golf course. Walk to your left round the edge of it until, where the boundary hedge starts to turn right and you are opposite a shelter, you will see a footpath sign. Follow this down to your left. Then in only a few yards turn to the right to find an iron swing gate. Go through and walk the length of the field – it is National Trust property – bearing right on approaching the end wall, and crossing to a stone stile by a cattle trough and gate. Climb the stile at a public footpath sign and go straight ahead along the edge of the University playing field to a stile by the second tree from the left in the opposite wall. The wall had collapsed at the time of writing, but it is to be hoped that the stile will be reinstated when it is rebuilt. Climb the stile and turn right along the tree-lined road for a few yards. Then climb an iron stile on the left immediately before the **dogs' home.** Keep to the right-hand hedge across the field, hoping the barking will die down as soon as you have passed, and climb the stile to the road at the side of a tiny wooden church.

Turn right, and just before the lay-by on the left, go down the drive on the left towards the farm. Keep to the right where the drive forks, and almost in line with the right-hand end of the house turn right along a track with a wall on your left. Climb the stone stile at the end, ahead of you. Then make for a wooden stile with stone steps, diagonally right. This takes you on to a track, which you will follow around the boundary of a chalet park, going through a gate. Just before the wood take the track to the left, at a footpath notice, and follow this round the field edge and through an iron swing gate. The path goes straight ahead now, through iron swing gates, until it reaches **Claverton Down Road** through a magnificent beechwood. There are views of Bath to be glimpsed on the way, down to the right. Turn right at the road, and walk along it. There is a tea garden, restaurant and pub if required here.

Go to the first turning on your left. This is **Tyning Road,** which you follow for only a few yards, to fork left into **Gladstone Road.** Continue along this to a path at the end, and go straight ahead with the school playing field on your right. Take the footpath ahead as the track swings round into the school, which leads you high above an old quarry. Cross the track at the end and go forward to the houses, **Monkswood,** and then down the signposted walled path to your left. Nearing the bottom of this you have a foretaste of the coming scene as you look over the wall to your right. Go through the gate to the road and immediately turn right down the stepped path. The whole village of **Monkton Combe** lies before you, clinging to the steep sides and nestling in the bottom of the valley of the Midford Brook. *The houses are mellow Bath stone, and the school fits in very well. Some of its buildings date from 1714. The church is to your right at the bottom, and is 19th century.* Turn left at the bottom of the steps and then right at the inn. You will then pass the 18th century lock-up. At the end of the road take the footpath ahead, to cross the mill stream, then a field, between fences, and the Midford Brook itself. This is a delightfully peaceful spot in which to linger. Turn left immediately after the bridge, over a stile, to walk in front of the houses. You will look down on the old mill which you passed earlier. Immediately past the last house at the road junction, climb the wooden stile in the hedge above you and cross the field to another. As you climb there are good views back across the hillside down which you have just come. Enter the wood and climb steeply for a short while. Then the path levels out and you climb a stile and continue straight ahead on the well trodden path, through a clearing, then forward on a track, rather devastated by tree felling operations at present, to emerge on the road by **Stoke Wood House.** Cross carefully and go down the tiny road exactly opposite. Take the first turning left, go forward at the junction, and bear right at the bottom, to reach the **'Hop Pole' Inn.**

Turn left round this. The entrance to their garden is round the corner. Then continue downhill to the road junction. Turn right, under the railway bridge, and if you wish to shorten the walk catch the bus back from here. If not, cross the river and continue uphill to the canal bridge. Take the track on the left just before it, and go immediately right over a stile, on to the towpath. Turn left and follow the canal. This section may be dry but it still has enough clear water in it to attract many dragonflies and you will probably find moorhen, mallard and swans along the canal. It is a really secluded spot and you think you are miles from everywhere, until an occasional train shatters the silence and you realize that river, canal and railway are all sharing this beautiful valley. There are views of the viaduct now to your left – you will remember having seen it from your descent into Monkton Combe. Then the river is close by, and shortly your path turns left to reveal one of the wonders of canal architecture – **Dundas Aqueduct,** built in the early 19th century, carrying the canal high above the river and the railway. It is a magnificent monument to the canal engineers and builders. At the end of the aqueduct is the basin where the Somerset Coal Canal used to join the Kennet and Avon. Walk right round the basin and behind the building to cross the canal by a decorated bridge, and continue on your way to **Bathampton.** There are two stone bridges to go under, on a bright day making mirror-like reflections in the water so that you see almost a full circle. Just after the bridge by the houses at Claverton you will see the magnificent Regency style **Warleigh Manor** on your right. What a scenically satisfying valley this one is!

Soon the **Dry-Arch Nursery** will come into view, and then the bridge which you crossed earlier. Just half a mile past this you will come back to **Bathampton.**

WALK 11 AVON VALLEY
SALTFORD, KELSTON, NORTH STOKE

DESCRIPTION:	Circular walk in River Avon Valley and south end of Cotswold escarpment, including two typical Cotswold villages.
MAPS:	OS 1:50,000 Sheet 172 (Bristol and Bath). OS 1:25,000 SP 66/76 (Bath and Keynsham).
DISTANCE:	10 or 7 miles.
TERRAIN:	Riverside and short stretches of hill walking. (No difficult climbing).
FOOD AND DRINK:	'Bird in Hand', 'Jolly Sailor', Saltford. 'Crown', Kelston.
TRANSPORT:	Bus: 338 or 339 from Bristol or Bath, to the top of Saltford Hill. Then go down Beech Road opposite the 'Crown' Hotel, bear right down the High Street, keep left of the 'Bird in Hand' and turn right up the approach to the cycle track where signposted.
START AND FINISH:	The Shallows, Saltford – Grid 686674.

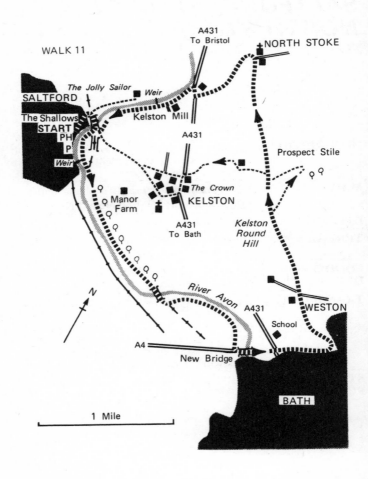

WALK 11

A431
To Bristol

✝NORTH STOKE

The Jolly Sailor — Weir

SALTFORD

The Shallows

START

PH

P

Weir

Kelston Mill

A431

Prospect Stile

Manor Farm

The Crown

KELSTON

A431
To Bath

Kelston Round Hill

River Avon

A431

WESTON

School

N

A4

New Bridge

BATH

1 Mile

Cars park free at Grid 686674, by public toilets, in the Shallows at Saltford.

Car passengers cut across the small field NE of the toilets and up the steps to the cycle track.

Cross the old railway bridge and after about 100 yards, look out on your left for the remains of the platform of the old Kelston Station and for surviving flowers escaped from its garden. It was from here that hundreds of racegoers used to climb the hill to Lansdown Racecourse.

Continue along the cycle track towards Bath (in a SSE direction) for 1¼ miles, skirting on your left the former home of the Inigo Jones family, **Kelston Park,** now a Methodist Youth Centre. *It was built about 1770 by John Wood Junior the famous Bath Architect and appears very plain in contrast with his Royal Crescent of roughly the same date.* On reaching the bridge across the river cross it and descend on the left on the far side and continue along the river bank to the 18th century **New Bridge,** associated with Ralph Allen the postal pioneer, marking the Bath City boundary.

Cross it and descend the steps on the far side.

Go to the right of the boating station and climb the steep well-defined path to the stile on the main **Bath–Bitton road, A431.** *A few yards down this road at 'Fairfield' the Emperor of Abyssinia and his family lived during most of the 1939–45 war.* Cross the A431 and take the path to the right of the large school to **Penn Hill Road,** and go ahead for 200 yards and into the recreation ground at the first entrance on the left.

Climb the second stile on the left and go straight up the steep slope to another stile. Climb it, and veer slightly right upwards and then along the contour between **Pendean Farm** and the lane rising from Weston village. After a further ½ mile along the well-trodden track, gently rising to the NW, it is only a ten-minute detour to the top of **Kelston Round Hill** and back. On your way you have a fine view of Weston Village, Primrose Hill and of Beckford's Tower on Lansdown Hill. *This 'folly' (1825) which is open to the public at summer weekends at a modest charge, contains interesting relics of William Beckford, the eccentric novelist.*

Continue north for ½ mile beyond the Round Hill where you reach a major track at right angles and there are 3 interesting alternatives.

(A) Go ahead up the hill for ¼ mile to **Prospect Stile** clearly visible on the skyline at 780 ft on the edge of Lansdown Racecourse. Stop here for perhaps the finest view in the whole Avon Valley with Weston-Super-Mare and beyond visible on a clear day and a glimpse of the west half of Bath. Across the racecourse is the memorial for the battle of 1643 when the Royalist leader Sir Bevil Grenville was killed. Return to the junction.

(B) Turn left at this junction (i.e. right, if returning from Prospect

Stile) and continue along this bridle track (NW) for one mile to **North Stoke** village. After viewing the church and old cottages descend the lane to the main road, A431. This is part of the road used by the Romans to transport troops and supplies through Bristol to Sea Mills (ABONA) whence they were shipped down the Avon and across the Severn Estuary to Caerleon and Caerwent. Turn right on the A431 for 100 yards, then left over the stile into the field beside the river. Follow it upstream to Kelston Mills to see the annealing towers of the once-flourishing brass industry. Continue along the river to a point a few yards east of the railway bridge where there are steps to take you up to the cycle track. Turn right to reach your starting point.

(C) Turn left at this junction, then left again after 200 yards down a stony lane for one mile to a point opposite the old forge in **Kelston Village.** Turn left on the main road, A431, past the 'Crown', noticing on many cottages the initials of the Inigo Jones family. At the bend in the road by the Tower House turn right and descend the lane, with a short detour to your left to see the 13th century church and ancient buildings of **Manor Farm** including a seven-bay barn and dovecote. Bear right past the remaining cottages and left through the farm gate and down through the fields to the railway bridge and back to the start.

WALK 12 AVON VALLEY BATH–BRADFORD ON AVON

DESCRIPTION:	The walk is soon in rural Bath, genuine countryside near the city centre, and then climbs steeply through fields to Combe Down. Surfaced paths and lanes drop down to the Kennet and Avon Canal, which is then followed for one mile. Riverside paths in the Avon and Frome valleys are taken and finally field paths into the Country Park at Bradford on Avon.
MAPS:	OS 1:50,000 Sheet 172 (Bristol and Bath); 173 (Swindon and Devizes).
	OS 1:25,000 ST 66/76 (Bath and Keynsham); ST 86/96 (Melksham).
DISTANCE:	10 miles.
TERRAIN:	Steep climb out of Bath, and then down to river valley and gently undulating countryside.
FOOD AND DRINK:	Coffee, lunch and tea at Combe Down. Pubs at Monkton Combe, Limpley Stoke, Freshford. Tea garden, cafe, restaurant, pubs at Bradford-on-Avon.

TRANSPORT:	Bus: Frequent service between Bath and Bradford and Trowbridge. Also limited stop service Bristol–Bath–Bradford–Salisbury.
	Train: Bristol–Bath–Freshford–Avoncliff–Bradford on Avon.
START:	Bath railway station.
FINISH:	Bradford on Avon.

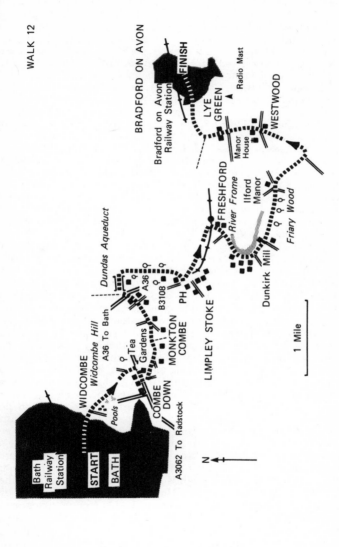

Many variations of this walk are possible by using buses or trains to or from various points, or by using the canal towpath which also links Bath and Bradford on Avon.

Leave **Bath** railway station and turn right to take a path under the railway, and across the river by a footbridge. Cross the dual carriageway road and turn left through the **Widcombe** shops. Take the second turning on the right, **Widcombe Hill,** and go uphill past the church. Soon on the right is Widcombe Crescent, a typical Bath crescent, and after this is Church Street, also on the right. Follow this to the church. The manor house is a few yards further on and is renowned as the home of two well-known authors. *In the 1740s Henry Fielding and his sister lived there, by consent of his patron, Sir Ralph Allen. It was here that 'Tom Jones' was written. In the late 1920s it became the home of H A Vachell, author of 'The Hill' and 'Quinneys'.*
Fork left at the church, along **Church Lane,** and you may soon have a glimpse of Prior Park House on the hill above. *This 18th century mansion was the home of Sir Ralph Allen, by whose inspiration and wealth the Georgian city of Bath was built. The house was designed in the Palladian style by John Wood the Elder, the architect of the Royal Crescent, and was completed in 1743. Since 1830 it has been a Roman Catholic public school.*

Where the lane becomes rough you can see the Palladian Bridge in the grounds of Prior Park. At the last house in the lane the path becomes enclosed between bushes and climbs uphill. In the field bear half left and make for the top corner, gradually bearing right to a stile by iron gates. You will probably want to pause for breath around here, after the stiff climb, and to admire the fine view of the city.

Ignore a stile on the left, and follow the stony path to a field. Cross this diagonally to the far corner, where turn right along a track to a main road. Turn right, soon passing the **Rockery Tea Gardens.** Coffee, lunches, and teas are available here from Easter to September. Take the first turning on the left, **Tyning Road,** and then turn left again into **Gladstone Road.** At the end this becomes a surfaced enclosed path, past playing fields, then small quarries, where Bath stone is cut. Cross the quarry access road and go downhill, along a drive, then an enclosed path, to join a lane. Turn right downhill, along the lane and soon enjoy a view of the Limpley Stoke Valley. Immediately after the first house on the right, take a surfaced path down to **Monkton Combe,** a 'wool' village, as are most in this stretch of the Avon valley, and now the home of another public school. The 'Wheelwright's Arms' is a short distance to the right if you want refreshment. However, the walk continues by turning left along the lane to a crossroads. Go straight across and down to the main road. The Bath and Bradford bus stops here at Dundas.

Cross to a stony lane and walk to **Dundas Wharf** on the Kennet and Avon Canal.

Follow the canal path to the right, across the aqueduct, continuing along the towpath. There is much wildlife on this tranquil stretch. In one mile, at the first bridge across, cross a gate on the right, and turn left to a main road. Turn right, down to cross the River Avon at **Limpley Stoke.** The Bath and Bradford bus also stops here. Walk under the railway, turn left along **Lower Stoke,** soon passing the 'Hop Pole' Inn and the Limpley Stoke Hotel. Both offer food, drink, and gardens. Continue to the bottom of the steep hill ahead, where you turn left under the railway to the riverside. Follow a path that is about halfway between the river and the railway gradually rising, until **Freshford Railway Station** is reached. A few trains call here for Bath and Bristol.

Cross the line by the footbridge and follow the lane to the village, which was once important in the wood trade and has some fine buildings. Turn left down to the Inn, which offers a restaurant and bar food. Immediately before the bridge over the **River Frome,** enter the field on the right through an iron swing gate. The path steadily climbs the bank on the right. At the top, follow the railings on the left downhill to fields and a road by a bridge over a river. Turn right along the lane, soon turning left at Dunkirk Mill Cottage along a rough lane.

Dunkirk Mill, built in 1795, was operated by water power from the small stream. Until recently it was derelict but has now been restored. At the entrance to the mill, turn left along an enclosed grassy track above the river and the weir in the Frome Valley. Where the path drops down, keep to the left hedge to a stony track. Turn left and immediately right along a grassy track into a field. Continue ahead into a wood. Bear left at a fork, down into a field. Follow the hedge on your right, making for the right-hand side of the house ahead. At the lane note Farleigh Castle further down the valley. *This was once a fortified manor house, built in 1369, for Thomas de Hungerford, the first speaker of the House of Commons.* Turn left along lane to Iford Bridge.

Turn right up the lane and soon take a stony bridleway on the right, which you follow to a lane. Turn left and in a few hundred yards by a bend, note the uneven surface in a field on the right. This is all the remains of Rowley, an abandoned mediaeval village. As a church comes into view as you walk along the lane, look for a stile on the bank on the right. Cross this and follow a path that is parallel with the lane. *Gradually a view unfolds on the right to show the Westbury White Horse, the Wiltshire Downs, and Salisbury Plain.* The path joins the lane again, through a wall stile to the right of **Westwood Church,** opposite **Westwood Manor.** *This manor, now owned by the National Trust, and open on certain afternoons, was built in the 15th century and is noted for its Jacobean windows and plasterwork, and for its topiary garden.*

Turn right to the 'New' Inn. Take the path alongside, into a field. Cross the centre of the field to a stile to the left of the television transmitter. Cross the centre of the next field bearing slightly left to a gate. Turn immediately right, to cross a stile. Turn left to a stile in the far right corner. Cross the lane to the gate opposite, where you get your first view of Bradford on Avon. Walk downhill, generally bearing left. About halfway down after crossing a stile in a wire fence, bear right, steeply downhill to a metal stile and a path near the canal, on the opposite side to the towpath. Follow this to a bridge, which you cross. Continue along a metalled road down to, and through the Country Park. Soon a footbridge over the river is reached (do not cross). The Tithe Barn and tea gardens are nearby. Bear left alongside the river and under the railway. Either continue to follow the river path to Bradford Bridge for the bus, or cross the car park to the Railway Station for the train.

For six hundred years Bradford on Avon was an important centre in the woollen industry. The town, with its steeply terraced weavers' cottages is packed with interest. The main attractions are the rare Saxon Church, the 14th century Tithe Barn, and a 17th century lock-up on the bridge.

WALK 13
STANTON PRIOR–PRISTON
MILL–STANTON PRIOR

DESCRIPTION:	This walk takes one through pleasant farmland, visiting the historic Priston Mill and the village of Priston.
MAPS:	OS 1:50,000 Sheet 172 (Bristol and Bath). OS 1:25,000 ST 66/76 (Bath).
DISTANCE:	8 miles.
TERRAIN:	Easy path and tracks.
FOOD AND DRINK:	'Ring o' Bells', Priston.
TRANSPORT:	Bus: 179 Bath–Paulton to Priston Turn. 129 Bath–Weston-super-Mare. 365 Bristol–Keynsham–Frome. 367 Bristol–Keynsham–Frome (Not Sun) to Marksbury. 368 Bristol–Keynsham–Radstock – Sun.
START AND FINISH:	Stanton Prior church, 8 miles south-east of Bristol

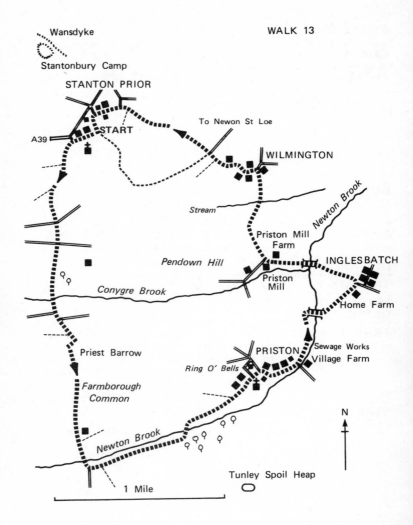

Wansdyke

Stantonbury Camp

WALK 13

STANTON PRIOR

START

To Newon St Loe

A39

WILMINGTON

Newton Brook

Stream

Priston Mill Farm

Pendown Hill

INGLESBATCH

Priston Mill

Conygre Brook

Home Farm

Priest Barrow

PRISTON

Sewage Works

Ring O' Bells

Village Farm

Farmborough Common

N

Newton Brook

Tunley Spoil Heap

1 Mile

74

From the church at **Stanton Prior,** go through the first field gate on the left, at the bend in the road. Cross the field to the green lane which leads to the first road. Cross this and continue along the lane to the second road to be encountered. Take the right-hand gate of the pair on the opposite side of the road, which leads on the right of way across the fields. Keeping the hedge on your left continue in the southerly direction to a stile in the next facing hedge, which involves crossing a negotiable barbed wire fence beforehand. Negotiating the stile takes one on to a field sloping down to a small stream at the bottom of a small but attractive valley. The stream is crossed at the far left-hand field corner. It can be rather soft and muddy after rain. The next field, taking the walker up the far side of the valley, is gained by a stile. Ascend this and a minor road is reached. Turn left briefly and then at the bend pass through into the field on the right, through the wooden gate the left hand of a pair of gates. Cross this field, and over wire, into the next field ahead. A small eminence, **Priest Barrow,** rises on the left and gives good views of the Cotswold edge in the vicinity of Lowdown Hill with its conspicuous clump of trees. Go over a stile in the hedge on the right; then turn left along the hedge to the next stile ahead at the end of the field; cross this. On the right of the next field rises Farmborough Common. Pass through the gate and find a stile set in the opposite hedge. From the next field gain the lane which leads to **Camerton** through a gate next to a house. Follow this lane a short distance down to the stream at the bed of the valley and turn into the field on the right-hand side of the stream over a stile by the side of a field gate.

Follow the stream, keeping it on your left, through four fields (gap, stile, gap) whence cross the stream, pass over a stile and mount a gently rising field to gain the end of the lane leading into **Priston** village. *From the afore-mentioned field the spoil heap at Tunley can be seen on the skyline to the south, a reminder of the once prosperous Somerset coalfield.*

Priston church gains attention by a fine gilded cockerel on the weather vane, and there is also in the village a pleasant pub where food is obtainable, the 'Ring o' Bells', set by a small village green.

Continuing the walk, go down the village street to **Village Farm.** Take the stile on the left, into the field, with the brook to the right. Go to the left of the sewage beds pass over two stiles, and keep the hedge to the right until reaching a concrete footbridge spanning the stream. Cross this, and mount the intervening fields towards Home Farm at **Inglesbatch.** Without passing through the farm go through a gate and turn left down the green lane to a gate. Two of the three poles ahead are waymarked down the field ahead to a stile in the hedge to the right. Go over this and the concrete footbridge is just to the left at the point where streams from Priston and the Mill converge. Across the next field lies **Priston Mill,** across the bridge (ST 695615).

Priston Mill is well-known locally for its wholemeal stone-ground flour, ground on the premises, and is interesting to visit. A mill has been known on the site for over a thousand years, and a reference is included in the Domesday Book. It is still working and possesses a fine 25 ft diameter waterwheel, installed in 1850. The Mill is open to visitors from mid-March to the end of October, and on Sundays only in November. It is part of Priston Mill Farm estate, and there is a farm shop, open from mid-March to mid-December.

From the Mill take the well-defined track leading straight up the hillside to the north by the first gate on the right out of the road, then through two gates into a large field at the top of the hill. Cross this in a nearly direct lane to a stile set in the far hedge overlooking the next valley. This field is frequently arable so please cross in single file, when this is the case. Descend the slope, cross the brook to a stile on the far bank and mount the opposite field to **Wilmington,** using the stile at the top of the field, and a further stile leading on to the road. The route from the Mill to Wilmington is virtually in a direct northerly line.

The track leading to the top of the hill from the Mill is not marked on the current (6/82) 1:25,000 Pathfinder map as a right of way (green dashes) but a telephone conversation with the Mill/Farm proprietor of the Mill (9.6.82) has established the recognition by him of this tract as a valid route for the public. Damage to the gates has been suffered by the Mill/Farm owner, necessitating their replacement, so please respect the property.

Turn left at the road, past **Wilmington Farm** to the crossroads in ¼ mile from which descend the hill along the road back to **Stanton Prior.** *Good views of the valley down to Newston St. Loe College and its grounds are obtained from the vicinity of the crossroads and also of the prominent landmark of Stantonbury Camp.*

An alternative return to Stanton Prior from Wilmington which possibly involves marginally less road walking is to turn left at the crossroads and after ½ mile, turn right down a rough unsurfaced lane, which brings the walker directly into the village in the vicinity of the church.

WALK 14 THE MENDIPS
NORTH MENDIP CIRCULAR
WALK

DESCRIPTION:	An easy walk in a part of Mendip once well-known for coal-mining, and interesting for industrial archaeology.
MAPS:	OS 1:50,000 Sheet 172 (Bristol and Bath). OS 1:25,000 ST 65/75 (Radstock and Wellow).
DISTANCE:	6–7 miles.
TERRAIN:	At first a fairly level path alongside the old railway and stream, then through undulating country.
FOOD AND DRINK:	The 'Gus and Crook' at Timsbury.
TRANSPORT:	Bus: Bristol–Frome 365; alight at the Hallatrow Hill stop on the Hallatrow–High Littleton Road.
START AND FINISH:	Public Footpath sign on the Hallatrow–High Littleton Road, on the right-hand side going towards High Littleton, just before the bridge over the river Cam.

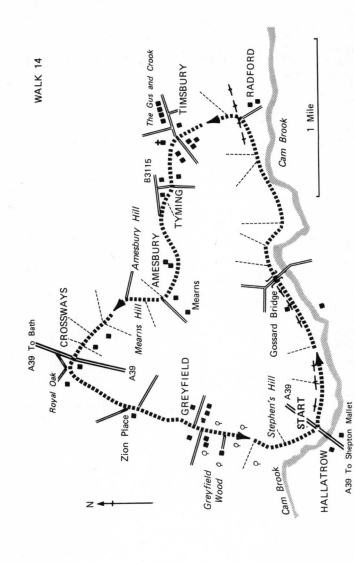

Car Parking – turn from the Wells Road along the B3355 Paulton Road and in about fifty yards park in a cul-de-sac on the right or a few yards farther along on the left.

Go through the gate and in about two hundred yards bear left up to a stile and turn right along the track of the old **Bath–Camerton railway line.** Continue in the same direction along the track to **Goosard Bridge.** In about a quarter of a mile the public footpath bears left over a stile and uphill to Langford Lane but at the moment there are no restrictions on the use of the old railway which is more pleasant and good for wild flowers. However, if the line is blocked it is easy to reach Goosard Bridge by following the footpath to Langford Lane and turning right.

On reaching Goosard Bridge via the railway track get up to the bridge by some steps on the left but should these be extremely wet and muddy go under the bridge, turn left and scramble up through the trees.

From the bridge go towards **Paulton,** but in a few yards go over a stile on the left into the sewage works. After about a hundred yards turn left round the edge of a fence opposite the sewage work's office and go along a narrow track and over a stile. Walk straight ahead for about fifty yards to a raised bank and bear right along this. *This is the bank of the old Bath–Camerton Canal which was constructed just before 1800 to transport coal from the North Somerset collieries, but closed in 1898 when competition from the railways made it no longer economic.* Follow this bank and where there is an old arch across the track of the canal, rather hidden by trees, bear left up to a stile and go to the right keeping to the hedge, over another stile and on to a gate on the left, climbing yet another stile to get out to a track. Bear right along this track for about fifty yards but look for a stile on the left and cross the grass to it. Continue in the same direction until you come to the lane leading into the hamlet of **Radford.** *Here you may divert to the* **Old Malt House Restaurant** *passing the remains of an old corn mill en route.*

To continue the walk, turn left on reaching the lane and follow **Mill Lane** uphill to **Timsbury.** This is a rough track and may be wet and muddy.

At the end of this you can go straight across the main road to reach Timsbury Church, but it is worth while turning right to look at an interesting old inn sign 'The Gus and Crook'. *The inn is dated 1704 and the sign shows the appalling working conditions once endured in the coalmines – the gus is the chain around the body of the boy and the crook attached it to the coal truck.*

From the inn go along Church Lane to the parish church, pass in front of it and turn right following along the wall of the church. Turn left, first right and then left again through the housing estate to find a public footpath sign and follow this to the fields. Make your way downhill, looking across to High Littleton and Paulton, and go through a gate and over two stiles to reach a lane. Turn left downhill and take a path on the right labelled 'To Amesbury'. M.R. 663587. Follow this to **Amesbury Hamlet** and go straight ahead to the fields, continuing in the same direction until you reach the third field where you turn sharp right and go out to the road and walk straight ahead up **Mearns Hill.** Take care as you turn left at the top on to the **Clutton–Timsbury Road** and also when you reach the A39 main Bath–Wells Road at **Crossways.** Go across the A39 and behind the 'Royal Oak' Inn, Free House, turning down the lane to **Zion Place.** Then turn left and first right passing **Greyfield Farm.** Look left for a view of Downside Abbey in the distance. *This abbey was started in the nineteenth century as the permanent home of the English Benedictine community of St. Gregory after they had been driven abroad by the Reformation, came back to England at the time of the French Revolution and finally settled in Somerset, building the well-known public school as well as the abbey.*

As you approach the bottom of this lane note a house on the left called 'Up the Gug', the gug being the passage leading into the coalmine.

At the next junction bear right and then in a few yards take a track on the left to reach Greyfields Wood. Turn left down a stony track through the wood and where this bears right continue straight ahead along a narrow and possibly muddy track to reach a stile. Exit into a field and go straight across to re-enter the wood. Almost immediately go left downhill to the stream, over the footbridge and turn right through the wood. This is a good place for wild flowers especially in Spring, but enjoyable at all times.

Go over a stile and in about fifty yards find another. From this bear left towards a wooden fence where yet another stile leads to a public footpath between the houses taking you back to the main road. Turn left to reach the B3355 where you will find a bus stop for transport to Bristol.

WALK 15 THE COTSWOLDS
CASTLE COMBE AND THE BY BROOK

DESCRIPTION:	A circular walk visiting several beautiful stone villages and hamlets lying under the southern edge of the Cotswolds – Castle Combe, West Kington, North Wraxall, Ford and Long Dean.
MAPS:	OS 1:50,000 Sheet 173 (Swindon and Devizes). OS 1:25,000 First Series ST 87.
DISTANCE:	10 miles.
TERRAIN:	River Valley to West Kington, level walking to North Wraxall then climbing steeply to drop to Ford and back along the river valley.
FOOD AND DRINK:	Two pubs (food) in Castle Combe. The 'White Hart' and the 'Castle'. The 'White Hart' at Ford – food.
TRANSPORT:	Large free car park above Castle Combe. Infrequent bus services from Chippenham or Bath (check times before setting out).
START AND FINISH:	Car park just off B4039 above Castle Combe. (or North Wraxall).

WALK 15

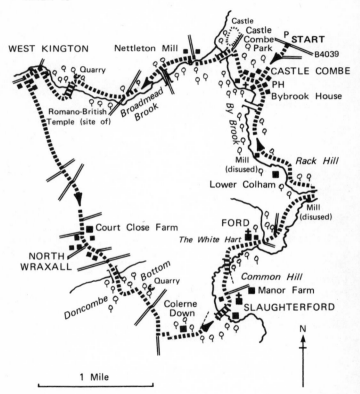

WEST KINGTON

Quarry

Nettleton Mill

Castle
Castle
Combe
Park

P START
B4039

CASTLE COMBE
PH
Bybrook House

Romano-British
Temple (site of)

Broadmead Brook

By Brook

Mill
(disused)
Lower Colham

Rack Hill

Mill
(disused)

Court Close Farm

FORD
The White Hart

NORTH
WRAXALL

Doncombe
Bottom
Quarry

Colerne
Down

Common Hill
Manor Farm
SLAUGHTERFORD

N

1 Mile

The walk can be started in either of two places. I prefer to start from North Wraxall because you will then end up in Castle Combe at lunch time where refreshment can be obtained at the two local inns, but you may also start at Castle Combe itself and that is how I have described the walk.

There is a large car park just off the B4039 road above the village, well signposted. Leave it by way of the steps and turn right down the lane. At the junction in 50 yards go right again and walk down the hill until the **Market Cross** is reached. Bear right around the front of the **Castle Hotel** and pass under the quaint house spanning the road facing you. The path goes left, then right and climbs steeply, finally ending in a stile into a wooded sloping field. Turn left and follow the wall on your left, emerging into an open field with views of the river below. Cross this field with the post and wire fence on your left until a stone bridge is reached. Here cross the river and follow the obvious path right and left through the trees with the river on your right until the ornamental stone and wrought iron gate is reached indicating the end of the Manor grounds. Pass through the gate towards the house and buildings forming part of what was once **Nettleton Mill,** one of a series of wool mills located along this river.

Turn left in 20 yards between the decaying buildings and follow the old track through the woods for $\frac{1}{2}$ mile with the river on your left until an old stone pack horse bridge is reached by a ford, ignoring a track coming in from the right just before reaching it. Do not cross the bridge but go through a small gate ahead on the right of the river. Immediately climb up into the field and take a track parallel to the river across a couple of fields. The path winds up and down but within sight of the river and eventually emerges through trees out into a lane by way of a small gate. This lane is the **Fosseway,** the Roman road which runs in a straight line from Bath to Cirencester. Turn left and proceed down the hill, but before the river is reached go through the gate on the right into a field and bear right around the edge of a steep wood with the river below to the left. This area is the site of a Romano-British Temple. At the corner of the wood do not turn right but cross the field ahead to the right of two trees, parallel with the river below to your left. The path leads down to a gate in front of woods and then bears left to the river's edge, crossing it by way of a stone bridge.

Carry on up the track, muddy in places, through the trees until it emerges into a lane. Here turn right, and carry on along it until the village of **West Kington** is reached.

Do not cross the bridge, but bearing left, climb the hill and take the first turning to the left by the sign post and marked as a 'No Through Road'. Proceed past **Pound Hill** and note the weather vane of an angler playing a fish on the roof of the farm buildings on the left-hand side. At **Woodbine Cottage** the road bears right and the tarmac surface abruptly ends, but the lane continues for another $\frac{1}{2}$ mile between typical Cotswold limestone walls until it passes into a field with the wall on the left only. Pass through into the next field and in 50 yards go through the opening in the wall on the left into the adjoining field. The path then continues along the edge of this field but now with the wall on your right until it reaches a lane. Cross straight over and climb the stile facing you.

In the field which drops away steeply you will notice a stone slab stuck vertically in the ground. This was originally a stone stile set in a wall which formed part of the parish boundary. The wall has long since disappeared but the stile still remains. Climb the field with a wall on your right and shortly before you reach the corner pass into the adjoining field on the right by way of a wire gate; then continue forward along the side of the field to the gate visible ahead. Cross the lane, the Fosseway again, climb another stile immediately opposite and go across this field with a post and wire fence on your right. In the corner another stile and stone slab leads out on to yet another lane and here turn right and walk along it for about $\frac{1}{2}$ mile until **North Wraxall** church is reached, ignoring another lane coming in from the left.

Turn left at the T-junction and drop down the hill through the village and climb the hill out. Just before **Southwood Cottage** and by the 'North Wraxall' sign on the right-hand verge, take the track leading off to the right and proceed out to the main A420 Chippenham–Bristol road and cross straight over to the track opposite.

Drop down 50 yards to a bungalow and take the right-hand path, not the more obvious left-hand one. The path is narrow and stony and drops steeply down into the woods and then crosses over a brook by a small stone bridge.

It bears right and forks. Take the left-hand fork which immediately starts to climb through the woods. At the crossing turn left and follow the path gradually upwards ignoring side paths. In 50 yards the track widens out and in a further 200 yards it forks. Take the right-hand fork which leads out of the woods into a field. Follow along the left-hand wall with the wood on the left until a lane is reached. Cross over and take the lane marked to Euridge.

The banks of this lane are bright in late spring with typical chalkland flowers including scabious, cornflower and a colony of pyramid orchids. Ignore the first field gate on the left at the bend, marked private, but continue along the lane and go through the next gateway on the left in 200 yards and proceed down the farm track with the wall on your right. Bear right and then left dropping down towards **Colerne Down** farmhouse ahead, ignoring tracks coming in from left and right. The hamlet of Slaughterford can be seen in the valley below. Past the farm the path splits into three ways and you should take the right-hand fork and drop down until a field gate is reached.

Pass through this gate and continue descending on the obvious track with the woods on your right. Pass through the opening in the hedge and continue straight ahead in line with the chimney on the skyline until the river is reached. Here turn left and follow the river bank for ¼ mile; then cross it by way of the footbridge over the weir. Now turn left and cross the water meadow with a hedge on your right in the general direction of farm buildings in the distance. Pass into a second meadow and continue in the same direction to reach a stile in the corner. Bearing slightly right, cross the next field towards the wood and over the river again by another footbridge over a weir. Cross the next field first along the river bank in the direction of houses ahead and then along the track by the side of the feeder brook, leading into a lane. Turn right and continue along this lane, past the 'White Hart' Inn and out to the A420 at Ford. Cross the road and turn right along the pavement towards Chippenham; then in 100 yards take the lane off to the left signposted to Castle Combe, by the side of **Bybrook Barn**. This lane climbs steeply through woods for ¼ mile until a stile on the right is reached, signposted to Long Dean.

The path across this field is visible following the contour of the field towards the woods. Follow the track to the woods with the hedge on your left and go through the gate to the right of an old barn. The path now becomes a sunken track, muddy at times but soon emerging on to a good surface. It leads to another bridge over the river and on into the hamlet of **Long Dean.**

At the junction take the track to the left of the letter box passing **Rose Cottage** on your right. Climb past the old mill on the left, and ignoring the turning off to the sewage works on the left continue climbing until a gate is reached with a footpath notice and a step-over stile to its right. Continue along the track ahead which soon opens out giving views up this quiet river valley. Then start gradually to descend through woods keeping the wall on your left until finally the tracks open out into a steeply sloping field and another step-over stile by the river. Cross this for the last time over another stone bridge. Here turn right and follow the river back into **Castle Combe** until the Market cross is reached, from where the walk began.

WALK 16 CHIPPENHAM MAUD HEATH'S CAUSEWAY

DESCRIPTION:	A circular walk out of Chippenham using most of the path created from a trust fund set up in the 15th century. Uses also the River Avon path and visits old villages and hamlets around North Wiltshire.
MAPS:	OS 1:50,000 173 (Swindon and Devizes). OS 1:25,000 First Series ST 97.
DISTANCE:	10 miles.
TERRAIN:	River Valley out of Chippenham with a climb to Bremhill dropping down to the River Marden and gently undulating back to Chippenham.
FOOD AND DRINK:	Good food at the 'Dumb Post' Public House at Bremhill, a choice of eating places in and around the Market Place in Chippenham with accommodation at the 'Angel' Hotel.
TRANSPORT:	Chippenham is on the main railway line from Paddington to Bristol and can be reached in $1\frac{1}{2}$ hours from Paddington. Bus services also from Bath, Bristol and Swindon. Car parking off the High Street, but best to use the Swimming Pool car park.
START AND FINISH:	Chippenham – Swimming Pool Car Park (Monkton Park).

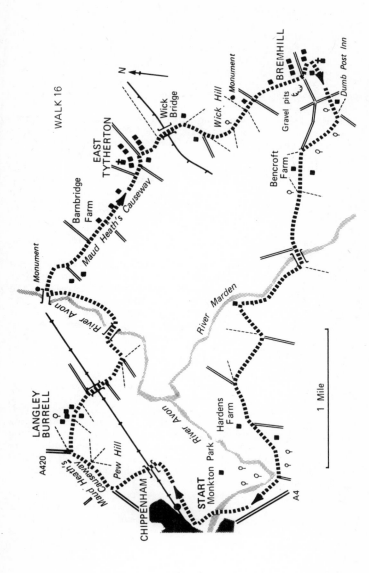

WALK 16

N

CHIPPENHAM

LANGLEY
BURRELL

A420

Maud Heath's Causeway

Pew Hill

Monument

River Avon

River Avon

START

Monkton Park

Hardens
Farm

River Avon

River Marden

A4

Barnbridge
Farm

EAST
TYTHERTON

Maud Heath's Causeway

Wick
Bridge

Wick Hill

Monument

BREMHILL

Gravel pits

Dumb Post Inn

Bencroft
Farm

1 Mile

This walk uses part of a footpath and causeway created as the result of a bequest by a widow of the parish of Bremhill, near Chippenham in 1474. Having been none too happy about the state of the roads between her village and the nearby town of Chippenham, where she would walk to on market days, Maud Heath left land and houses, the income from which was to be used to set up and maintain 'a highway and causeway from Wick Hill to Chippenham Clift'. The path was duly laid out and a causeway built where it crossed the River Avon and it exists to this day.

From the car park take the short road towards the College buildings; then turn right along **Cocklebury Road** until you arrive at the tree in the middle of the road. On the left, between the building and the railway line is a track, usually overgrown in summer but passable, which goes under a railway arch and out into a field. Follow the left-hand hedge of this field with the railway line on your left, until you climb a stile and emerge into a lane. Turn left and almost immediately cross over the main **London railway line,** noting, away to your right, the second bridge which will be crossed later on. The track now becomes a tarmac road and leads out to the main A420 road.

Turn right along the pavement which is in fact the first encounter with Maud Heath's causeway.

Continue along this pavement passing the industrial development and Parsonage Road, as far as the **Langley Burrell junction.** Here turn right and pass through the village until the **Old Brewery** and 'Brewers Arms' Public House are reached, and then turn off right along the lane signposted to Peckingell and Tytherton Lucas. *The causeway itself continues straight on at this point and you may carry on along it if you wish, picking up the walk again at Kellaways Bridge. A far more pleasant walk however is the one now described which uses the path alongside the river.*

Continue down the lane and cross over the railway by means of the footbridge referred to previously. At the next junction turn right, passing **Dolphin Cottage,** and then in 20 yards turn left down a pebbled track, keeping the overgrown hedge and ditch on your right. At the bottom of this field the track bears left and passes through a gap in the hedge over a bridge spanning a wide brook. Do not use the old bridge a few yards before this gap as the surface timbers are rotten. Immediately turn left through a gate into another field and follow along the bank of the brook towards the old war-time pillbox visible at the end of the field.

In the right-hand corner of this field is a concrete footbridge over the River Avon, here a gentle meandering stream full of roach and chub which can sometimes be seen in the clear water on sunny days. Cross the bridge and turn left along the riverbank path and keep on it for about three quarters of a mile until **Kellaways Bridge** is reached.

You will have now rejoined **Maud Heath's causeway** and perhaps the most spectacular part of the path. The river at this point would frequently burst its banks in winter, and as a result a causeway was built either side of the bridge, 17 arches on one side and 45 arches on the other, to allow the river to be crossed on foot in the dry.

A pillar was set up here in 1698 to commemorate Maud Heath's generosity, with sundials in three faces and a warning that the traveller should haste on since 'He (the sun) shall return again but never thou'. Heed also the warning to 'Injure me not'.

Turn right now and walk away from the river along the causeway, passing the tiny **church of St. Giles,** and noting the fine old **Kellaways Farm** building at the end of its drive on the bend. The path now continues along this lane for a mile or so, ignoring turnings to left and right, first on one side of the road and then on the other, until the village of **East Tytherton** is reached.

Turn right here. Note the triangular monument recording the 500th anniversary of the Causeway, and proceed on the Bremhill Road. Before you start to climb up **Wick Hill** you will pass over the course of the old **Wilts and Berks Canal,** now sadly little more than an overgrown ditch. The path winds up the hill and ends at an inscribed stone in the hedge on the right of the road. On your left, through a stile by the pine trees, can be seen a monument to the good lady, set up in 1838, a good spot for a rest and a picnic after the climb.

Returning to the road turn left and continue out to the T-junction. Straight ahead will be noticed a stile in the hedge and the way lies straight across this field to a stile in the far hedge. Here bear half right to the field corner visible 50 yards ahead; then proceed with the hedge on your right until a stile is reached before the field drops away. Cross this stile and you will notice below to your left a track over a brook, which, once crossed, starts to climb towards the last cottage. Before passing through the gate on to the drive note the old gravel workings away on the right.

At the road turn left and proceed through **Bremhill village.** Opposite the **Post Office,** just before the green, is a small gate on the right leading into the churchyard. The path skirts around the edge of the burial ground with a wall on the right until the main entrance door to the church is reached. Here leave the church grounds by the gate and cross the field bearing slightly left of the Georgian house to a stile in the corner of a field. Cross this field with the tree-lined hedge on your right and make for a stile in the far corner to the right of the white cottage, and drop down into the lane with the 'Dumb Post' Inn ahead.

The name suggests more than the pillarbox painted on the inn sign, and tradition has it that this was the site of a gibbet in far off days. Certainly the inn itself is old, and was used as an overnight stop in the days of the coaches. Snacks are usually available here. The way lies behind the inn along the lane signposted to Studley. Dropping down the hill, go through the gate into a field on the right just before the second house, called Foxways, and cross this field above the wood on the left. Pass through a gate into a second field and climb steadily in the direction of the farm buildings on the skyline towards a small gate visible in the trees and leading out to a lane. Turn left here and passing **Bencroft Farm,** drop down Bencroft Hill, again crossing the line of the canal between Wharf Cottage and Stanley Bridge Farm.

Ignore the turning to West Tytherton and in 50 yards the bridge over the **River Marden** is reached. Cross the bridge and immediately turn right through the gate and follow the riverbank through three fields until the ruin of **Scotts Mill** is reached. Here go slightly left along the bank of the dried up mill race through the gap in the hedge, over a brook, then forward through the gate facing you about 20 yards away. There is a footpath across the fields to the right but like so many it is seldom used and difficult to follow. The easiest way is to proceed straight up this field on the vehicle track into the next field and drop down to a gate on to the line of the former Chippenham to Calne branch railway line.

Here turn right and follow this track crossing two fields and finally turning left over the cattle grid and down the concrete road, just before the electricity pylons. After passing **Hardens Farm** in about half a mile, enter the first field by the gate past the farm and cross it diagonally in a left-handed direction to a gate in the far corner. Proceed through the next couple of fields keeping the hedge on your right, finally crossing a stile by the corner of a concrete building. The tarmac path then starts to climb, but turn off right along the road – Long Cross – fronting the housing estate. Proceed to the end of the road; then follow the tarmac path past **The Butts** into St. Mary Street. Turn right where signposted down into **Monkton Park,** crossing the river by way of the footbridge; then cut diagonally left across the park aiming for the visible path leading uphill from the swimming pool, which will return you to the car park and the starting point.

WALK 17 CHIPPENHAM
A RIVERSIDE WALK TO LACOCK

DESCRIPTION:	A linear walk along the River Avon between Chippenham and Lacock. Picturesque cottages and bridge at Reybridge and the National Trust Village of Lacock with its abbey and photographic museum.
MAPS:	OS 1:50,000 Sheet 173 (Swindon and Devizes).
	OS 1:25,000 First Series ST 97.
DISTANCE:	3 miles.
TERRAIN:	Gently undulating riverside meadows.
FOOD AND DRINK:	3 Inns at Lacock. The 'George'. The 'Carpenters Arms' and the 'Red Lion' – all serving food. Also 'King John's Hunting Lodge' for teas etc. In Chippenham there is a choice of eating places in and around the Market Place and the Angel Hotel is also a Motel.
TRANSPORT:	Plenty of car parking in Chippenham off the High Street, and behind the 'Red Lion' in Lacock. An hourly bus service links Chippenham and Lacock. Chippenham is on the main Paddington-Bristol railway line and can be reached in $1\frac{1}{2}$ hours from Paddington.
START:	Chippenham.
FINISH:	Lacock.

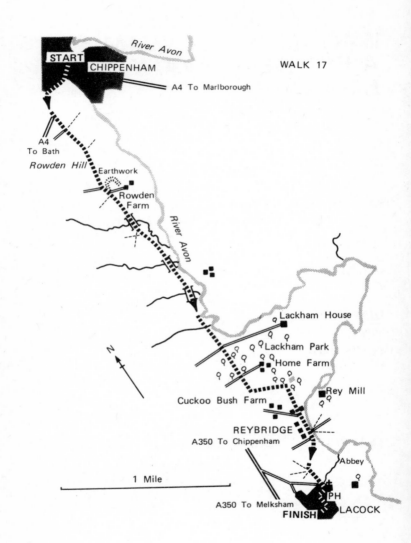

River Avon

START CHIPPENHAM

WALK 17

A4 To Marlborough

A4 To Bath

Rowden Hill

Earthwork

Rowden Farm

River Avon

N

Lackham House

Lackham Park

Home Farm

Cuckoo Bush Farm

Rey Mill

REYBRIDGE

A350 To Chippenham

1 Mile

Abbey

A350 To Melksham

PH

FINISH LACOCK

From the **bridge** over the River Avon in **Chippenham,** turn left along the **Bath Road** taking the right-hand pavement, as the left-hand one stops in 100 yards. At the junction with **Ivy Lane** cross straight over and proceed up the hill until the road bends and **Charter Road** comes in on the left. 50 yards on from this road you will notice an unmade lane going off to the left behind a house. Go down this lane and in 100 yards or so, just past the footpath which comes in from the right, there is a gap in the hedge facing you, with a cattle grid.

Go through this gap and cross this field and the next along the track until you reach another cattle grid where the track bears left down to **Bowden Farm.** Do not go down to the farm but climb over a stile high in the hedge immediately after the bend and cross this field more or less in the middle. The stile in the far hedge cannot be seen, but if you take a line slightly to the right of the electricity pylon visible on the skyline, you will spot it as you approach the hedge. Cross the small field to the bridge ahead over a brook and continue along the right-hand hedge ignoring the first stile ahead, but go through the barred opening into the next field.

Now cross this field taking a left-hand diagonal line to a gate in the post and wire fence to the right of the willow tree. Actually this is another bridge spanning a brook and is the only way over it. The next stile is visible on the edge of the river bank which you will be following for the next ½ mile or so.

Cross the next field and a double wire fence again by a concealed bridge over a drainage brook. After crossing the next field, leave the river at the horse shoe bend and make for the double fence ahead with a small brook flowing in front of it. There is a stepping stone to help you cross it and a small gate in the second fence which brings you into a field rising in front of you, a good stopping place for a picnic. If you look back towards the way you have come you will have a view back to Chippenham, with the spire of St Paul's church prominent.

Climb up this field between the war-time pillbox and the hedge, and you will emerge through a wired up kissing gate into the entrance drive to **Lackham College of Agriculture,** a County Council training school for farming and horticulture. Cross over the drive and through the gate into a field. The path is straight ahead down the side of the wire fence towards a spinney of conifer trees. Cross two stiles either side of a track; then go around the right-hand edge of this field making for a stile visible on the far side beneath the pine trees at the end of a copse.

Enter this copse and follow the path which leads out to another estate road opposite a small lake. Turn right here and walk along the road out past the quaint lodge – note the chimneys and the unusual method of construction.

Continue straight ahead down the road into **Reybridge** and take the path immediately ahead between the two cottages facing you after passing the bridge on your left. This is a tarmac footpath across the field, and when the kissing gate is reached at the far end, turn left and drop down past cottages and along the side of the ford into **Lacock.**

There is plenty to see in Lacock. The Abbey is usually open from Easter and if you are interested in photography the Fox Talbot Museum is a must. The village is owned by the National Trust and there are three excellent inns where refreshment can be obtained. The bus back to Chippenham leaves from the shelter near the George Inn.

WALK 18 WILTSHIRE
WESTBURY CIRCULAR
WALK

DESCRIPTION:	The first half of the route is beneath the Wiltshire downs escarpment, along relatively level tracks and paths, and through the interesting old villages of Bratton and Edington. A fairly steep climb follows up on to the open hills with wide vistas of Salisbury Plain, and views from the edge akin to cliff top walking. There is a sparse bus service between Westbury, Bratton, and Edington which may be useful to those with limited time.
MAPS:	OS 1:50,000 Sheet 183 (Yeovil and Frome); 184 (Salisbury and The Plain). OS 1:25,000 ST 85 and ST 95 (First Series).
DISTANCE:	From the railway station the longer route is 12 miles, the shorter 8½. From the town the longer route is 10½ miles, the shorter 7.
TERRAIN:	First half level below hills. Fairly steep climb to hills above Edington, then level and steady downhill.
FOOD AND DRINK:	Pubs at Bratton and Edington.
TRANSPORT:	Bus: Sparse bus service between Westbury, Bratton and Edington; Bristol–Westbury (and Salisbury). Train: Bristol–Westbury.

From the **Railway Station** turn left along the approach road and at the bend climb the steps up to the road. Turn right, then immediately left along a lane. Take the next lane on the right and follow this lane and road to the main **Trowbridge road.** Bear right to the **Market Square,** and cross this to the 'Lopes Arms'. *From the car park or bus stop in the town, enter High Street. Follow this in an easterly direction, past the shops, and turn left at the end. Bear right along Maristow Street to the Market Square and the 'Lopes Arms'.*

All Saints Church, on the south side of the Square, dates from the 15th century and stands on the site of a wooden Saxon church. Inside are several memorials to notable local families and a stone bench on the west wall for the use of the old and infirm in the days before church pews.

From the 'Lopes Arms' enter the churchyard, and take the centre path across, and then a short path into a road. Take the left fork, **Bitham Lane,** and follow this path to a road. Turn right uphill to a crossroads. There is a pottery opposite. Then turn left on to **Bratton Road** (B3098), noting the view over the fields towards Trowbridge and Bradford on Avon. At the cemetery the first sight of the White Horse carved in the hillside comes into view. Much later on, the walk takes you to the top of this ancient monument.

According to legend, the original chalk carving, an odd elongated creature, commemorated King Alfred's victory over the Danes at the nearby battle of Ethandune (Edington) in 878. It is more likely that it first appeared about 1700, as a fake to substantiate a legend. It was replaced in 1778 by the present figure, cut by the Chief Steward of Lord Abingdon's estate at Heywood, no doubt to improve the outlook from his master's house, seen in the distance towards Trowbridge.

Just past the end of the roadside pavement, $\frac{1}{2}$ mile from the pottery, fork left along an unsurfaced track. Follow this for $1\frac{1}{2}$ miles in the same general direction until it joins a metalled lane. The buildings away on the left are the **Cement Works.**

Continue straight on for 200 yards, where you cross a stile on the right, into an enclosed path to another stile. In the field follow the hedge to the top corner. *The view opens out to include Devizes, Roundway Down, and, in the far distance, another White Horse at Alton Barnes.* Continue along another enclosed path to a road. Go straight across, up Bury Lane. At a facing thatched cottage follow the lane to the left, which soon bears right as a surfaced path. At a

WALK 18

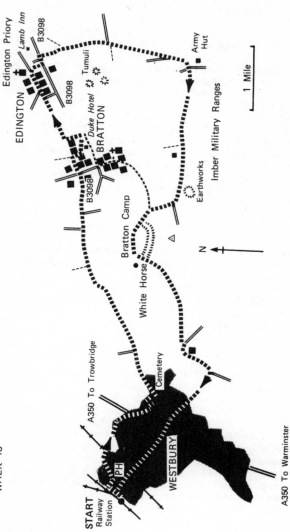

crossing path, by an old chapel, turn right. Cross the road to a path opposite, where, in a few yards, turn left. At a road, follow the pavement and path opposite, to the side of the **Duke Hotel** at **Bratton** where there is a restaurant, bar food, and a beer garden.

For the shorter walk: *Walk along the road towards Westbury. Take the second turning on the left,* **the Butts** *and bear right at an old school.* Where the road dips, take the enclosed path on the left to a gate into the churchyard. Do not enter, but follow the path on the right. At a stile on the left, do not cross it, turn right along enclosed path to a stile. Follow the path along a belt of trees, and continue to more open country. Walk upwards along a track indented in the hillside. At the top, follow the fence on your left to a stile and on to a sunken track. Turn right.

For the longer walk: From the war memorial, by the Duke, turn left along Sands Lane, which soon becomes a surfaced path between walls. At a road, cross to the drive opposite, and go through an old mill yard and garden, following a stream, then uphill to a stile. Continue with the hedge on your left across three stiles towards the large church ahead. The third stile is about 50 yards to the right of the corner gate. At a lane turn left and soon at a road junction turn right, passing several thatched cottages.

Soon fork left to 'Inmead' at a 'No Through Road' sign. Bear left and immediately take the surfaced path on the right which leads to **Edington Priory.** There are two pubs at the other end of the village, ½ mile away, but not on the route of this walk.

William Cheyney, whose family owned Edington Manor, was Bishop of Winchester and Royal Chancellor at the time of the Hundred Years War with France. He founded and endowed a college for a warden and twelve priests, and built a church and living quarters for them. This later became a monastery for the Order of St Augustine. When the monasteries were dissolved, the land passed to Thomas Seymour. The buildings fell into disrepair, but within the last century the Priory Church has been fully restored. The monastery garden and fish pond are behind the priory, but are not open to the public.

Leave the priory by the main gate, turn half right and walk to the grass triangle. Cross this to follow the surfaced path behind houses. At the road junction turn left along main road. Take the first turning on the right, a private drive by the post office and soon fork left, along an enclosed path. Cross the stile and walk up through a fairly steep narrow valley. At the top go through the gate and continue straight along the downland track until a large barn is reached. Here turn right, and then left along a green lane. On joining a metalled road, close to an Army hut, turn right, and soon left along another road. *Glimpses of the wide view from the hills can be seen on the right. The land on the left is vast and open, being part of the Imber* **Army Ranges.** *The roads which cross it are opened to the public for only a few weeks every* *year. In the middle stands the deserted village of Imber. As well as being an up-to-date battle field, it is also the most likely site for the battle which King Alfred fought against the Danes in 878. After about one mile along this road is a large clump of trees on the left, over an old earthwork.* ¼ mile further on, go through a gate on the right and follow the enclosed track to open ground. Continue along the sunken track for ¼ mile.

(The shorter walk joins at this point)

At the head of the valley on the right, climb the grass bank on the left, by the easiest slope, to a road. If this indistinct path is missed, continue along the track to the road, where turn left uphill, cross the road and follow the grassy path below the earthwork to reach the top of the lower earthwork on the very edge of the hill. Follow this to the top of the White Horse. This is **Bratton Castle,** an Iron Age hill fort. The view from these heights is truly extensive, encompassing the Mendips, the Cotswolds, the Welsh Mountains, and the Marlborough Downs, with many towns and villages laid out before you.

Continue around the edge of the hill towards Westbury, passing the topograph and the seats to a stile. Follow the path beside the wire fence on the edge of the hill. At the small wood bear left then right along the raised side of the field to a road. Turn right downhill. Soon after a bend to the right, take the rough lane on the left past a barn. In ¼ mile go through the iron swing gate on the right. Then follow the hedge over the hill into the enclosed path to the second crossing road, **The Butts.** Turn right, then left by **Snappersnipes** to a main road. Turn left and follow the road round bends to the top of **Haynes Road.** Turn right to the bus stop, High Street, and the car parks. For the Railway Station, continue along Haynes Road to the bottom, then follow Station Road and Station Approach to the station.

WALK 19 WELLS
WELLS–PRIDDY–WESTBURY –EBBOR GORGE–WOOKEY HOLE–WELLS

DESCRIPTION:	A circular walk through some of the best Mendip scenery in the Wells area, but it is not too strenuous.
MAPS:	OS 1:50,000 Sheet 182 (Weston-Super-Mare and Bridgwater). OS 1:25,000 ST44/54 (Wells and Wedmore); ST45/55 (Cheddar).
DISTANCE:	13 miles.
TERRAIN:	Gentle climb to the top of the Mendips, then fairly level, descend to Draycott and then up again to Ebbor Gorge.
FOOD AND DRINK:	The Inns in Priddy Village.
TRANSPORT:	Bus: Bristol–Wells 376; alight at the New Street stop in Wells.
START AND FINISH:	West Mendip Way post, New Street, Wells.

WALK 19

Follow the **West Mendip Way** along the Lovers' Walk, turning right through the school grounds and on to **Ash Lane**. Continue straight across, following the public footpath between the houses up to **Milton Hill**. Walk straight ahead until you reach the **Mendip Way Post** just beyond the side of the quarry and at this point leave the 'Way' and bear right down the farm road to **Model Farm**. At the farm turn right along the concrete track and then left into the field. Go straight across to the lane which runs from the Old Bristol Road to Wookey Hole. Turn left into the lane and in about fifty yards look for a partially hidden stile on the right-hand side. Go over the stile and uphill keeping towards the right-hand side. On reaching the top of the slope ignore the gate straight ahead but go through the gate a few yards away on the left. Follow the right-hand hedge to the top of the field and through the gate to join the track leading uphill. Part of this may be very muddy during a wet spell. *The slope on the right-hand side is excellent for flowers, including the early purple orchid, spring potentilla, common rock rose, and centaury.* Go through the gate at the top of the track and make diagonally left uphill to a small gate on the left-hand side; bear left through the gate and along the ridge, pausing to look at the view of Wells, Wookey Hole and the plain of Somerset beyond. At the end of the field turn right over a stile, and go across two fields to **Dursdon Drove.** This is one of the old drove roads used especially for moving sheep to and from the Priddy area. Turn left and walk along the drove until you find a **West Mendip Way post** on the right-hand side. The farmer has recently obtained a diversion, so the entrance is now farther along the drove than the position of the original footpath shown on O.S. maps. Rejoin the 'Way' and follow the waymarking signs to the **Priddy–Wookey Hole Road.** Turn right and walk into **Priddy village** where food and drinks are available at the inn. *Priddy is the oldest farming village on Mendip and a sheep fair is held on the Green on the nearest Wednesday to August 21st. This dates from 1348 when the Black Death caused the fair to be moved from Wells. Note the old hurdles on the Green, no longer actually used for the fair but kept as a symbol of the wool trade. As you approach the corner of the Green note the old cottage, 1739 Thomas Reeves. You will probably see cavers on the Green preparing to descend the well-known swallet of Swildon's Hole which is close at hand.*

Do not cross the Green but turn left along the Westbury Road until you find the **West Mendip Way Post** on the left-hand side of the road. Enter the field and go diagonally right, over a stile and across the next field to the lane. Turn left and go straight across the road at the end and into the field ahead still following the West Mendip Way. Keep near the left-hand side through two fields, then over a stone stile and continue in the same direction over three more stone stiles. *Look back at the Priddy and Ashen Hill Bronze Age*

Barrows which are probably the best known round ones in the Mendip area. At the end of May it is worthwhile diverting into the field in front of the clump of trees when you reach the top of the slope to look for the green winged orchid which is now much less common on Mendip. *As you make your way downhill, look at the view ahead, Glastonbury Tor to the left, the Somerset Levels in front and to the right Steep Holm, Brean Down, Cheddar Reservoir and Crook Peak.* Go over the stile at the bottom of the slope and across to the next one, but after climbing this, leave the West Mendip Way and go downhill to a gate ahead with the sign, Rodney Stoke Nature Reserve. Go through the gate and downhill on a track between the two stretches of wood, another excellent place for flowers, and straight down the field keeping to the right of the house at the bottom and get over into **Wood Lane.** From here bear right into **Scaddens Lane** and out to the main **Wells–Weston road.** Take care as you turn left as this is a twisting and much used main road. Here you may catch the 126 bus back to Wells if you wish to shorten the walk. As you walk uphill along the road look for a track on the left-hand side as the road bends at the top of the slope. This may be rather overgrown but will take you round to **Hill Farm** avoiding the main road. At the end of the track turn left towards Priddy, looking out for quarry lorries, but at the first junction bear right and continue past **Old Ditch Farm** to **Back Lane.** Follow this lane and at its end turn left uphill taking the first lane on the right, **Mares Lane.** Go through the gate at the end of this, across two fields and on entering the third bear right downhill to a gate into a lane. Turn left and where the lane terminates, enter the field and go straight ahead up the valley. Go through a gate and keep going uphill, bearing right at the top to reach the Priddy–Wookey Hole road. Turn right downhill and as you go towards the Ebbor Nature Reserve note two stones in a field on the right. These stones are reputed to mark the boundary of the original Royal Forest and once a deer was outside this the local inhabitants had the right to hunt it. Hence the local name of 'Deerleap'.

When you reach the **Ebbor Nature Reserve Car Park** look for a stile and go over it into the gorge. Go down through the gorge and from the exit gate continue in the same direction and then turn left into Wookey Hole village. Refreshments may be obtained at the **'Cave' Restaurant.**

Pass the Caves entrance and bowling green and go straight ahead up a track signposted Lower Milton, over a stone stile and bear right through three fields to a lane. Turn left past **Myrtle Farm** and in about quarter of a mile find a stone stile on the right. Go over this and on through three fields back to **Model Farm.** Go through the gate and then bear diagonally right away from the farm towards the wood and out of the field on to Milton Hill. Walk towards the left-hand hedge and follow the metalled lane downhill crossing Ash Lane and on past the entrance to the **Blue School.** Pass the end of **Mounterey Road** and on reaching **Lovers' Walk** turn left back to the starting point. The bus stop to return to Bristol is a few yards uphill. Turn right downhill to reach the **Union Street Car Park.**

WALK 20 THE QUANTOCKS HOLFORD–KILVE–QUAN-TOCKS–HOLFORD

DESCRIPTION:	A walk along a short stretch of Quantock coast, and a ridge of the hills. The coastal area is comparatively little known.
MAPS:	OS 1:50,000 Sheet 181 (Minehead and Brendon Hills). OS 1:25,000 ST 03/13 (Quantock Hills); ST 04/14 (Watchet).
DISTANCE:	10 miles.
TERRAIN:	Both coastal and hill-walking; moderate ascent up on to ridge; easy going throughout otherwise.
FOOD AND DRINK:	Afternoon tea: 'Coombe House' Hotel, Holford Combe. Recommended small cafe and general store at Holford Post Office; sale of local OS maps.
TRANSPORT:	None.
START AND FINISH:	Holford Green.

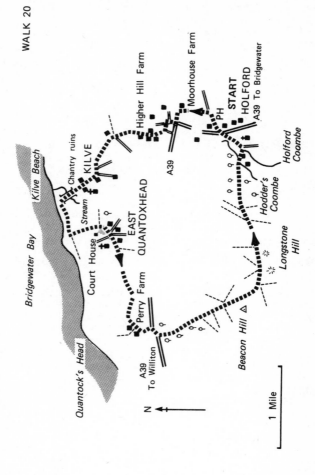

Bridgewater Bay

Quantock's Head

Kilve Beach

Chantry ruins

KILVE

Stream

Court House

EAST
QUANTOXHEAD

Perry Farm

A39
To Williton

Higher Hill Farm

A39

Moorhouse Farm

PH

START
HOLFORD

A39 To Bridgewater

Holford
Coombe

Hodder's
Coombe

Longstone
Hill

Beacon Hill △

N

1 Mile

From Holford post office, turn left along the A39 briefly for 50 yards; then turn right into a minor road, **Green Close.** Follow this for ¼ mile, and turn left into a green lane. This leads in a further ¼ mile to **Moorhouse Farm.** Turn left along the farm road back to the A39. Immediately bear right into a minor road; go left at the crossroads and turn right at the next junction. At the sharp bend in the road a footpath (stile) goes to the right; follow this path through the fields near the houses to join the lane at a gate. Walk down the cul-de-sac to its end at **Higher Hill Farm.**

Go through a gate into the field, with the stream on your right. Cross the field, along the valley to a gate leading into a lane. Turn right towards the disused cottage. Just before this and without crossing the stream, turn left into a rough field. Keep the hedge close to the right and to a stile in the bottom corner. In the corner of the next field is a further stile. Cross the next field to a gate. Go through this and immediately turn left through a gate into a rough track. Follow this to a road and turn right, over a stone bridge, to the road junction. Turn right into **Sea Lane.** Follow this towards the sea, passing the church and ruins of the chantry on the left. A road bridge over the river takes one to the car park for **Kilve Beach.** At the far end of this car park, by the toilets, go left through a gate over the river and proceed to the beach.

The foreshore here has a number of points of interest; it is noted for conger eels, shows a very striking folding of the strata, and was the site for an attempt at oil recovery from the shales at the beginning of the century, an enterprise abandoned due to the high sulphur content of the oil. Fossils known as St. Keyna serpents are also found, St. Kia being a local saint who allegedly turned snakes into stones. The area of Kilve was popular with smugglers, the chantry and church tower being used for the storage of brandy kegs.

From the beach turn up to the Ministry of Defence hut, **HMS Heron.** Go over the stile and along the coast path, enjoying the fine coastal views westwards to Minehead and Selworthy Beacon. After one further stile, a small beach is reached, access by a flight of steps and a signpost to E. Quantoxhead and Kilve Church. Turn inland, pass a small stone structure on your right, a disused lime kiln, and go along a broad grass track well fenced on both sides, over a small stream by a bridge, and through a kissing gate. Go on along the next stretch of path, through another kissing gate with a stream on the left to the bottom of the gardens of Court House. This has been in view since joining the cliff path. Turn right up by side of gardens. There is a notice 'To beach' here, and a post with a yellow arrow waymark. Go up to the church, with the stream on the right. A rough track leads up to **East Quantoxhead** village.

The village contains Court House, in possession of the Luttrell family of Dunster Castle for about 700 years and still occupied by them; a fine church with carved benchends; thatched cottages and a pretty duckpond. The gardens of Court House are finely landscaped and planted.

On leaving the village, take the right-hand road fork, and follow it for ½ mile, when the road takes a sharp left-hand bend. A grass track continues on forward. There is a signpost to W. Quantoxhead and Perry and a yellow arrow waymark. Follow this over a small rise into a shady sunken lane. Go down this, through a stile or gate into the field where there is a yellow arrow. Go across to the next stile or gate into a field. There is a view down the small dry valley right to the sea. Keep around the edge of the field with the hedge on your left to a gate into a rough track. (Note, if doing this walk in reverse, it is the central gate of three). Follow the rough lane down to **Perry Farm.** There is a signpost with a circular disc carrying a white arrow on black ground; and also engraved on the post is 'E. Quantoxhead'. Turn left up the farm track to join the A39 at **Perry.**

Turn right for ¼ mile along the A39 to a track on your left, marked, 'Footpath to W. Quantoxhead avoiding main road'. Enter this, pass through an iron gate, and take the right hand of two small coombes to commence the return to Holford on the hills. Ascend the combe until the remains of a low wall are seen on the right. Follow a path by the side of this wall until a major track is reached. This ascends on to the main ridge with an iron fence bordering a plantation on the right. Pass by the wood and ascend to the summit of **Beacon Hill,** the triangulation pillar of which lies ahead. After pausing to admire the view, go along a short way to a major crossing of tracks. Turn left and follow the track along the crest of **Longstone Hill,** so named after the Long Stone, a Bronze Age standing stone re-erected in the 1960s. The track descends, with the deep wooded valley of **Hodders Combe** on the right, after about 1½ miles, on to the tarmac road from Alfoxton Park. Turn right to regain **Holford Green.** Note the fine views along the coast from the ridge, along which several alternative pathways are possible.

Afternoon tea is obtainable from Coombe House Hotel in Holford Combe. The hotel adjoins the old mill with the mill wheel extant. Here the Quantock Weavers functioned until the 1970s. At Holford the trees of Holford Beeches are well-known. The churchyard contains the grave of F. Norton, composer of 'Chu Chin Chow'. Alfoxton Park was the home of the Wordsworths in 1797 and is now an hotel. As the road from Alfoxton Park is joined at the end of the descent from Longstone Hill, note the ancient dog pound, given to the village in 1982, as described on the inscribed plaque.

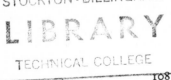